CONTENTS

Map iv

Acknowledgements vi

Introduction 1

Fundy Isles 5

Passamaquoddy Bay and St. Croix River 29

Fundy Coast 41

St. John River 63

Chignecto Bay and Tributaries 83

Northumberland Strait and Gulf of Saint Lawrence 97

Miramichi Bay and River 125

Chaleur Bay 135

Glossary 151

Bibliography 153

Index 154

New Brunswick's Lighthouses

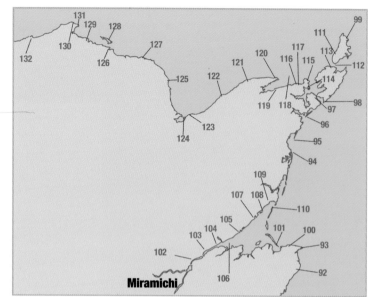

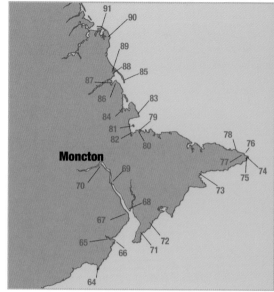

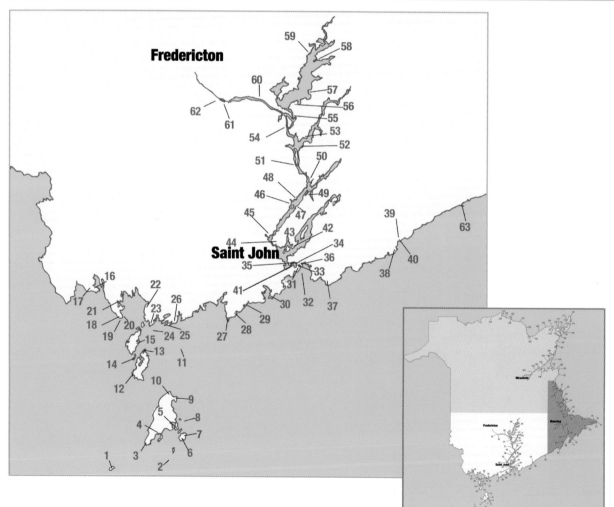

LIGHTHOUSES
OF
NEW BRUNSWICK
• PAST AND PRESENT •

Kraig Anderson and Kelly Anne Loughery

NIMBUS
PUBLISHING LTD

Nimbus Publishing Limited
3731 Mackintosh St, Halifax, NS B3K 5A5
(902) 455-4286 nimbus.ca

Printed and bound in China

Design: Jenn Embree

Library and Archives Canada Cataloguing in Publication

Anderson, Kraig
Lighthouses of New Brunswick : past and present / Kraig
Anderson and Kelly Anne Loughery.
ISBN 978-1-55109-915-6

1. Lighthouses—New Brunswick—Guidebooks. 2. Beacons—New
Brunswick—Guidebooks. 3. Lighthouses—New Brunswick—History.
4. Beacons—New Brunswick—History. I. Loughery, Kelly Anne II. Title.

VK1027.N48A53 2012   387.1′55097151   C2011-907635-7

Nimbus Publishing acknowledges the financial support for its publishing activities from the Government of Canada through the Canada Book Fund (CBF) and the Canada Council for the Arts, and from the Province of Nova Scotia through the Department of Communities, Culture and Heritage.

1. Machias Seal Island
2. Gannet Rock
3. Southwest Head
4. Seal Cove Breakwater
5. Grand Harbour (Ross Island)
6. Long Point
7. Gull Cove
8. Great Duck Island
9. Swallowtail
10. Long Eddy Point (Grand Manan)
11. Southwest (Southern) Wolf Island
12. Mulholland Point
13. Head Harbour (East Quoddy)
14. Cherry Island
15. Leonardville
16. Spruce Point
17. Mark Point
18. St. Andrews (Pendlebury)
19. Navy Bar
20. Tongue Shoal (Sand Reef)
21. Chamcook
22. Midjik Bluff
23. Green's Point (L'etete Passage)
24. Bliss Island
25. Pea Point
26. Lighthouse Point (Beaver Harbour, Drews Head)
27. Point Lepreau
28. Dipper Harbour
29. Chance Harbour
30. Musquash Head
31. Negro Point
32. Partridge Island
33. Saint John Harbour Beacon
34. Saint John Coast Guard Base
35. Digby Pier
36. Reed's Point
37. Cape Spencer
38. Quaco Head
39. St. Martins Visitor Information Centre
40. St. Martins Breakwater
41. Swift Point (Green Head)
42. McColgan Point
43. Bayswater
44. Sand Point
45. Belyeas Point
46. Glenwood
47. The Cedars
48. Oak Point
49. Shamper's Wharf
50. Palmer's Landing
51. Hampstead Wharf
52. Lower Musquash Island
53. Hendry Farm
54. Gagetown
55. Jemseg
56. Robertson Point
57. Fanjoys Point
58. Cox Point
59. McMann Point
60. Bridges Point
61. Oromocto Shoals
62. Wilmot Bluff
63. Martin Head
64. Cape Enrage
65. Anderson Hollow
66. Grindstone Island
67. Hopewell Wharf
68. Fort Folly Point
69. McFarlane Point
70. Outhouse Point
71. Pecks Point
72. Barnes Point (Woody Point)
73. Fort Monckton
74. Indian Point Range Front
75. Indian Point Range Rear
76. Cape Tormentine Outer Wharf
77. Cape Tormentine Range Rear
78. Cape Jourimain
79. Pointe du Chêne Range Front
80. Pointe du Chêne Range Rear
81. Shediac Island
82. Shediac Wharf
83. Caissie Point
84. Cocagne Range Front
85. Bouctouche (Buctouche) Bar
86. Dixon Point Range Front
87. Dixon Point Range Rear
88. Pointe à Jérôme Range Front
89. Pointe à Jérôme Range Rear
90. Richibucto Head (Cap Lumière)
91. Richibucto Beach
92. Pointe Sapin
93. Point Escuminac
94. South Tracadie
95. North Tracadie
96. Pokemouche
97. Portage Island
98. Big Shippegan
99. Miscou Island
100. Preston Beach
101. Fox Island Ranges
102. Newcastle (Lime Kiln Bank)
103. Oak Point Range Front
104. Grant Beach Range Front
105. Grant Beach Range Rear
106. Sheldrake Island
107. Grand Dune (Grandoon) Flats Range Front
108. Hay Island
109. Lower Neguac Range Rear (Tabusintac)
110. Neguac Gully
111. Goose Lake
112. Harper Point (Miscou Harbour)
113. Black Point
114. Marcelle Point
115. Pokesudie
116. Caraquet Range Front
117. Caraquet Range Rear
118. Caraquet Island
119. Pointe à Brideau Range Rear
120. Maisonnette
121. Grande Anse
122. Stonehaven (Clifton Breakwater)
123. Belloni (Salmon) Point
124. Bathurst Range
125. Petit Rocher
126. Belledune Point
127. Little Belledune Point
128. Heron Island
129. Dalhousie Wharf
130. Douglas Island
131. Inch Arran (Bon Ami)
132. Campbellton

◆ Lost lights are marked in grey ◆

◆ See also alphabetical index on page 154 ◆

ACKNOWLEDGEMENTS

A huge thank you to the following for their valued assistance:

The Canadian Coast Guard personnel who over the years have allowed countless hours of access to files, photos and to the lighthouses themselves as well as answering a myriad of questions: Bill Parker, Barry Nisbet, Tommy Curran, Ralph Hartlen, Dave Carlson, Claire MacLaren, Mona Gautreau, and of course Larry Wilson, whose own love of lighthouses helped to fuel the spark within us all here in the Maritimes.

The private lighthouse owners who graciously shared their history and knowledge of their lights as well as allowed us access: Ken Tower, Charles Stewart, John Audet, Bob Campbell, Gordon and Carla Burns, Kurt Lavigne, Andre and Yvette Maillet, and Joe Leger.

Individuals and journalists who supplied photos or helped to spread the word of our need of same: Michel Forand, Ralph Eldridge, Doug and Edith Andrews, Allan Roy, Charles Stewart, Bill Clarke, J-G. Landry, Jacques Godin, Tim Jacques of the *Campbellton Tribune*, and Alan Cochran of the *Moncton Times and Transcript*.

Others who have assisted us in gathering information or gaining access to sites: Jean Matheson (Library and Archives Canada), Julia Thompson (Provincial Archives of New Brunswick), Catherine Reid (New Brunswick Public Library Service), Linda LeFevre, Michael Leggett, and Barry Murray.

And finally, a dept of gratitude to those individuals, often strangers, who kindly ferried us out to offshore lights: Germain Maillet, Phillip Higgins, Joe McIntyre, and Brian Durelle.

INTRODUCTION

New Brunswick is the largest of the three Maritime provinces in Canada and home to the third-largest collection of lighthouses in the country. Originally part of the British holding known as Nova Scotia, New Brunswick became an independent colony in 1784, one year after the Loyalists arrived en masse following the American Revolution. They settled in the southern portion of the province, primarily the City of Saint John (the oldest incorporated city in Canada) and up the rich fertile valley of the St. John River. The first lighthouse in the province was established in 1785 on Partridge Island in Saint John harbour, and the fourth tower in that location still serves traffic entering the port city.

Southern New Brunswick forms the western shore of the mighty Bay of Fundy where the highest tides in the world are found. Twice daily over one hundred billion tonnes of water enter and leave the bay creating these record tides and carving out marvels in stone along its shores. Several islands dot the southern portion of the bay giving the area its collective nickname the "Fundy Isles." It is here that many of New Brunswick's most significant lighthouses can be found, including Gannet Rock, a wave-swept sentinel located thirteen kilometres south of Grand Manan and one of only nine octagonal wooden towers left in New Brunswick, as well as Machias Seal Island, the only staffed lightstation remaining in the Maritimes.

The largest of the Fundy Isles is Grand Manan, a place steeped in lighthouse history and culture. It is home to four active lighthouses, including lovely Swallowtail, which welcomes those arriving by ferry from the mainland. Swallowtail is another of the nine octagonal wooden towers and one of the few

lightstations remaining in the province. Also just offshore but accessible at low tide is the decaying Grand Harbour Lighthouse, an example of what happens when our lighthouses are abandoned.

Another of the major Fundy Isles is Campobello, as well known to Americans as it is to those in New Brunswick thanks to its most famous resident, President Franklin Delano Roosevelt who summered on the island with his family. Roosevelt Campobello International Park is the only park of its kind in the world and serves as caretaker for the nearby Mulholland Point Lighthouse, another octagonal wooden tower. At the other end of the island is Head Harbour, or East Quoddy as it is known on the other side of the border. Little introduction is needed as this beautiful lighthouse is not only the oldest wooden lighthouse in all of Canada but is also one of the best known and most photographed.

The area west of Campobello and nearby Deer Island is known as the Passamaquoddy Bay, named after the native people who were its original inhabitants. The beautiful town of St. Andrews lies along its shore, and it is here that the octagonal wooden lighthouse of the same name can be found, now under the stewardship of the St. Andrews Civic Trust. The area was once home to a number of lighthouses that are referred to in this book as "Lost Lights."

Several lighthouses dot the coast between St. Andrews and Saint John, where the mighty St. John River ends at the world-famous Reversing Falls Rapids. The St. John River, so named by Samuel de Champlain in 1604, rises in the state of Maine and travels approximately 725 kilometres to its terminus at the falls and Saint John Harbour. Along the last 100 kilometres can be found eastern Canada's only system of inland lighthouses, of which twelve still stand and six are still active. These are primarily small wooden "salt shaker" lighthouses scattered along the bucolic shores of what has been called "The Rhine of North America." They were built during the era of the grand riverboats and were usually located at or near wharves and acted as leading lights to guide the riverboat captains. They were cared for by nearby farmers, and in many cases it was the women of the families who performed the twice-daily task of tending to the lights.

At the head of the Bay of Fundy, where the tides are the highest, are Chignecto Bay, Shepody Bay, Cumberland Basin, and the Petitcodiac River. Although Cape Enrage is the only active lighthouse on any of these waterways, there are several others to be found, including Grindstone Island, the only buttressed hexagonal lighthouse in the province, and little Anderson Hollow, the most-travelled lighthouse in New Brunswick, having been moved a total of four times since it first sat at the end of a wharf in Waterside.

New Brunswick is Canada's only officially bilingual province, and it is along the East Coast and North Shore that the French population can be found. Known as Acadians, they have a rather turbulent history that is celebrated with pride, and no matter what language you speak, most will welcome you with open arms.

The Northumberland Strait divides New Brunswick from beautiful Prince Edward Island and boasts some of the warmest salt water north of the Gulf of Mexico. At 12.9 kilometres, the Confederation Bridge is the longest bridge in the world spanning frozen waters. When it opened in 1997, the bridge made obsolete the ferries that had previously connected the two provinces, along with the area's lighthouses. One is the beautiful Cape Jourimain Lighthouse, a wooden octagonal tower with graceful architectural appointments that have earned it a Federal Heritage Buildings Review Office (FHBRO) designation. It sits within the confines of the popular Cape Jourimain Nature Park.

Several small range lights guide fishing vessels into a number of villages along the shore from the sandy beaches of Shediac on up to Point Escuminac, the end

of the Northumberland Strait. Point Escuminac is the only concrete "apple core" lighthouse in New Brunswick. North of Point Escuminac is the Miramichi Bay and River, and the Gulf of Saint Lawrence. Several islands dot the entrance to Miramichi Bay and were once home to a number of lighthouses, probably the largest concentration of "Lost Lights" found within these pages. Several others were found along the northern shore of the bay and into the lower reaches of the Miramichi River. Some of these are still standing but have been moved from their original locations and are now privately owned and maintained in various degrees of authenticity.

From Miramichi up is what is known as the Acadian Peninsula, an area without existing lighthouses until one reaches Shippagan and the Big Shippegan Lighthouse, an octagonal wooden tower located about one kilometre out a long sand bar. (The current spelling for the town is "Shippagan," but historically and in marine records "Shippegan" was used.) Following the main road across the island of Lamèque you cross a bridge onto Miscou Island. At the very northern tip of the island—and the province—is the Miscou Island Lighthouse, another of the wooden octagonal towers. This lighthouse site was closed for a number of years due to environmental issues, but in 2009 it was completely renovated and reopened in time to kick off the Congrès Mondial Acadien, a massive gathering of people of Acadian descent. The Miscou Lighthouse houses a third-order Fresnel lens and divides the Gulf of Saint Lawrence from the Bay of Chaleur and the North Shore of New Brunswick. While the newest lighthouse in the province, Pointe à Brideau, is located in Caraquet along with a set of range lights, there is little remaining of this area's lighthouses until Dalhousie and the unique Inch Arran Lighthouse.

While many of the lighthouses that once stood on the East Coast and North Shore of New Brunswick have been lost, those that still stand have been altered very little with the exception of a few that are now private. Such is not the case along the Bay of Fundy where many of the original lighthouses, those wooden structures with attached dwellings, have been replaced with modern concrete or fibreglass towers. Some of these old wooden structures were lost at the hands of Mother Nature, but sadly, others were lost at the hands of our Coast Guard, who in the 1960s and 70s were mandated to discontinue or replace them.

New Brunswick lighthouses were originally under the control of the commissioners of light houses, with separate commissions later appointed for the Bay of Fundy and the Gulf of Saint Lawrence. Starting in 1788, a tonnage duty was imposed on shipping, and the resulting income was kept in a Lighthouse Fund, used to construct and operate lighthouses in the colony. With Confederation in 1867, the department of marine was formed to oversee lighthouses at the national level with a marine agent in Saint John responsible for lights in the province.

So why in this day and age of global positioning satellites and other technological advances should we be concerned with seemingly antiquated aids to navigation? To this we say that we are part of the Maritime provinces, with a seafaring history in fishing, shipbuilding, or lightkeeping, and to lose a lighthouse is to lose not only a part of our history but a part of ourselves. A colleague and fellow lighthouse enthusiast puts it best when she says that for centuries lighthouses have taken care of us, and now it is our turn to take care of them.

We have endeavored within these pages to share not only those lighthouses still standing in the province but historical images of what they once were as well as those "Lost Lights" that are gone forever. Several mast or pole lights kept by keepers were also used, but these we have not included. (A surviving example of this type of light can be seen at Musée des Pionniers in Grande-Digue.) For those readers who would like to use this book as a travel guide, you will find not only the GPS coordinates for each light, but also directions to those still existing—which is not to say that all are accessible. Some are offshore and require a boat or helicopter to view while others are on private property (such lighthouse sites should only be visited when one is invited to do so by the owner). This is where you will find the accompanying icons for each light useful. A complete list of icons and their meanings follows at the end of this section. And keep in mind that in the Bay of Fundy area, it is imperative to be mindful of the tides or you can find yourself stranded for six hours.

It is our sincere hope that this book will help you learn about and visit the lighthouses of New Brunswick. If anyone has additional information on a lighthouse in New Brunswick, past or present, we encourage you to contact us through the website lighthousefriends.com, where you can also find lists of known keepers for all existing lighthouses.

LEGEND

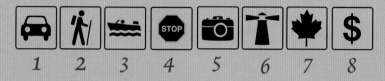

1   2   3   4   5   6   7   8

1 – Drive to the lighthouse with a short easy walk.

2 – A hike of some distance or rugged terrain involved after parking.

3 – Accessible/viewable only by boat.

4 – Privately owned or no public access available. Do not proceed without permission.

5 – Lighthouse and/or setting are particularly scenic.

6 – Tower or site open to the public with various facilities available.

7 – Historic significance attached to the lighthouse or site.

8 – Fee involved (sometimes seasonal).

Aerial view of Machias Seal Island. (Head keeper Ralph Eldridge)

FUNDY ISLES

1. Machias Seal Island

As tiny Machias Seal Island is located roughly nineteen kilometres from the nearest points in Canada and the United States, it is understandable that both countries have claimed sovereignty over it. In terms of navigation, the island was more crucial to Canadian interests, as vessels bound to and from the ports of Saint John and St. Andrews passed nearby, but the United States was reluctant to relinquish the associated prime fishing grounds.

In response to the continued petition of the chamber of commerce of Saint Andrews, the government of New Brunswick allocated £750 in 1831 for a light on Machias Seal Island. Two octagonal wooden towers and a keeper's dwelling were built in 1832, and John Pendlebury was appointed the first keeper. The two lights, each employing eight lamps and reflectors, prevented the site being confused with either the revolving light at Gannet Rock or the single fixed light at Head Harbour. During 1857, the lights were fuelled by 700 gallons of seal oil and 207 gallons of porpoise oil, which was more expensive but necessary in cold weather.

As Machias Seal Island was frequently shrouded in fog, the keeper was supplied with a four-pound signal gun in 1841 to serve as a fog signal. In 1843, a supply of provisions was cached on the island, and a large tank was erected to store rainwater for "shipwrecked Seamen and Emigrants."

By 1869, one of the two lighthouses was worn out, and Messrs. Clarke and Stackhouse were contracted to construct a new tower. The light from a powerful third-order Fresnel lens was first exhibited from this new lighthouse on November 6, 1869. Though the brighter light was appreciated, it also created a problem. Mariners could often see only the more powerful of Machias Seal's two lights, or would see two lights but think the dimmer light was from the keeper's dwelling, and would thus conclude they were off West Quoddy, where a single third-order light was displayed.

A steam fog-whistle was established on Machias Seal Island in 1873, with James Ackroyd as its engineer. The following year brought an end to Keeper John Conley's thirty-plus years of service

Two lighthouses were used on Machias Seal Island until 1915. (Canadian Coast Guard)

Puffin and Machias Seal Island Lighthouse. (Head keeper Ralph Eldridge)

Travel Instructions: Machias Seal Island can be visited on puffin trips offered by Sea Watch Tours (506-662-8552) from Grand Manan Island, and Bold Coast Charter Company (207-259-4484) from Cutler, Maine.

Established: 1832 (present tower 1915)

Position: 44.50183 N, -67.10114 W

Light: White flash every 3 s

Tower Height: 18.3 metres

Focal Plane: 25 metres

Description: White octagonal tower, red-roofed lantern

service on the island, along with the much shorter service of James Ackroyd and his replacement J. H. Crosby, who resigned after just six months because his family was unwilling to reside on the island. Wright Edmundson was then placed in charge of both the fog signal and the lights, but he left the island after a year when the marine department refused to increase his salary. Marine agent John H. Harding filed the following report after his visit to Machias Seal to remove Edmundson and deliver the new keeper, Alexander Eddy: "I regret to say that I found this station in a very unsatisfactory condition. The keeper, being a slovenly and untidy person, had allowed the whole station and its appurtenances to present a very neglected and disorderly appearance. The boiler had been burnt and was leaking badly."

In 1877, eight years after the new tower commenced operation, a contract was awarded to George Armstrong to construct a new companion tower. Unfortunately, the Chance Brothers Fresnel lens intended for this lighthouse was destroyed at the department's warehouse in Saint John during the Great Fire of 1877. Another lens was ordered from the same establishment, and the new lighthouse, an octagonal tower situated 59 metres southeast of the west tower and standing 16.2 metres from base to vane, commenced operation on November 1, 1878.

In 1915, an octagonal, 18.3-metre-tall, reinforced concrete tower that remains in use today was erected near the middle of the island and commenced displaying a distinctive flashing white light. No longer needed, the two wooden towers were eventually demolished. A new dwelling was built on the island in 1923 for the keeper, allowing the older dwelling, which had been housing both the keeper and his assistant, to be remodelled for the assistant. The two dwellings on the island today are of more recent origin.

In 1944, the government of Canada made Machias Seal Island and the surrounding waters a bird sanctuary. The island is home to the largest nesting colony of puffins on the Atlantic coast south of the Gulf of Saint Lawrence.

Today, Newfoundland and British Columbia are the only two Canadian provinces that still have staffed lighthouses, with one exception: Machias Seal Island. Though Machias Seal Island Lighthouse has been automated for several years, the department of foreign affairs covers the cost of maintaining keepers on the island "for sovereignty purposes."

2. Gannet Rock

Named after the black and white gannets that formerly nested there, Gannet Rock lies thirteen kilometres south of Grand Manan Island and is one of numerous rocks and ledges that litter the western side of the entrance to the Bay of Fundy. Murr Ledges are found between Gannet Rock and Machias Seal Island, while a dangerous rock called Old Proprietor is located eleven kilometres northeast of Gannet Rock.

A bill was approved in 1824 calling for the establishment of a revolving light "upon one of the islands or rocks near the southeast coast of the Island of Grand Manan," and the commissioners of lighthouses examined the area in 1825 to ascertain the best site for a lighthouse. Part of their investigation reportedly included leaving rafts of logs on various rocks and ledges over the winter to determine safe locations. In 1830 the commissioners gave £1,000 "to be applied towards building, establishing and maintaining a floating light off the Old Proprietor, near the Island of Grand Manan, provided it may be found practicable to carry it into effect, and if not, the sum to be applied towards building a Light House on the Gannet Rock."

Construction of Gannet Rock Lighthouse won out, and work on the exposed rock, which rises to a height of twelve metres and is about ninety metres in length at high tide, was carried out in 1831. Crawford, Gray & Purvis were paid £630 for erecting a lighthouse and dwelling, and David Hogg was given £155 for providing the lantern. The original lighthouse stood 12.6 metres from base to vane, and each face of the octagonal tower was painted with a black and white vertical stripe. When the light was first lit in December of 1831, the lantern was fitted with red glass, but as this greatly diminished the power of the light, the characteristic was changed in 1843 to eleven seconds of white light followed by nine seconds of darkness. The flashing characteristic was achieved by a shade that was raised and lowered by a weight-driven mechanism, wound every six hours.

Original Gannet Rock Lighthouse with its distinctive black-and-white striped daymark. (Canadian Coast Guard)

The first keeper of Gannet Rock Lighthouse was Captain Thomas Lamb, who received £165 per year, from which he paid an assistant. E. G. Miller took over when Captain Lamb was transferred to Quaco Head in 1835. Keeper Miller served at Gannet Rock until 1837, when he drowned while rowing back to the station after procuring a fresh supply of water on nearby Kent Island.

Lauchlan Donaldson inspected Gannet Rock Lighthouse in 1839 and reported that it was "a fearful place in storms." During a gale the previous winter, several shingles were washed off the lower part of the tower, and Donaldson concurred with Keeper Jonathon Kent's opinion that only the iron braces and chains that had been put in place in 1838 to anchor the tower to the rock saved it from being swept away. As Kent was responsible for one of the few mechanical lights in New Brunswick, lived on a mere spot of rock where grass never grew, and was cut off from all contact with the world, Donaldson suggested that a wall of cut stone be built around the tower for protection and that Kent receive an increase in salary.

In 1840, the station was given a signal gun, and a chute was chiselled into the rock so the keeper could easily launch and take up his boat. A granite wall was

Recently heightened Gannet Rock Lighthouse, atop a new concrete foundation and topped with a new lantern, 1906. (Provincial Archives of New Brunswick)

built around the lighthouse in 1845 to render the station "perfectly secure" and bring comfort to the keepers at the "desolate and dreary station."

Walter McLaughlin was appointed keeper of Gannet Rock Lighthouse in 1853 and spent the next twenty-seven years at the lonely outpost. Fortunately, he wrote a journal.

July 9, 1856. Mr. Pettingell and 3 other carpenters landed with 12½ thousand shingles last night.

July 9, 1867. We discontinue the light today and begin to take down the old lantern.

August 1, 1867. We lit the new light and were well satisfied with it. A new lantern and fourth-order Fresnel lens for Gannet Rock were acquired in 1866, but the attempt to install them that year was defeated by a period of rough seas and unfavourable weather.

October 11, 1871. We have detected a strong smell of burning buildings, and I am of the opinion that some large city such as New York or Boston is burnt.

October 18, 1871. The boat came today and brought news of the burning of Chicago.

In 1880, Keeper McLaughlin was transferred to the newly constructed Southwest Head Lighthouse, and Oliver A. Kent, an assistant keeper at Gannet Rock for many years, was appointed his successor. A house of refuge for the keepers was built in 1884 in case a fire broke out on the rock.

In 1894, a cotton powder cartridge, exploded every

Gannet Rock Lighthouse in 1987: freshly painted and still staffed. (Canadian Coast Guard)

twenty minutes, replaced the fog gun, which had been fired every hour. A small building was erected at the south end of the station to house the electric firing apparatus. Pilots and shipmasters were "loud in their praise" of this new fog signal, whose reports were sharper than those of the gun.

Elsie Clark lived on Gannet Rock with her father, Keeper Lincoln Harvey, from 1898 to 1904. When Elsie was in her late nineties, she related the following to Deborah Daggett:

[The house] was timbered up like a ship—made with beams just like the beams of a ship—two beams came out on the floor about two feet. I remember sitting on them in front of the stove. The stove was off a vessel, the Gertrude E. Smith, I think, and was made of thick iron—it burned soft coal. The kitchen was about eighteen feet long…The living room wasn't so big and from there was a big thick door into the lighthouse. Stairs went up from the kitchen. Upstairs was one big bedroom. From that room you went down a long hallway to the

Travel Instructions: Gannet Rock Lighthouse is best seen by boat.

Established: 1831

Position: 44.51031 N, -66.78136 W

Light: White flash every 5 s

Tower Height: 22.9 metres

Focal Plane: 28.2 metres

Description: Octagonal tower with black and white vertical stripes, red lantern

Gannet Rock's 1905 second-order Fresnel lens was removed in 1967 and donated to the Grand Manan Museum, where it is on permanent display.

lighthouse. There was a big bedroom on the second floor of the lighthouse and two big closets. Then on the third floor of the lighthouse was another smaller bedroom.

In 1905, the wooden octagonal tower was increased in height, placed atop an octagonal, concrete, 3.7-metre-high wall, and topped with a new red, circular lantern. These improvements brought the height of the tower to 27.4 metres. A second-order Fresnel lens produced two bright flashes every fifteen seconds with a lamp that burned petroleum vapour under an incandescent mantle.

Work on a new keeper's dwelling commenced in 1906, and the following year day labourers constructed a new fog alarm building to house a five-inch diaphone plant. The rectangular wooden building was placed on the southern end of Gannet Rock, and its horn pointed due south.

An electric lighting plant was installed at the station in 1913, a year before the outbreak of the First World War, and amazingly that conflict would reach remote Gannet Rock. The four-masted schooner *Dornfontein* departed Saint John on its maiden voyage on July 31, 1918. Just after the vessel passed Grand Manan, a German U-boat surfaced and fired two shots across its bow. The schooner's crew was taken aboard the submarine while the Germans looted the vessel and set it ablaze. After being fed a dinner of bully beef and rice, the crew of the *Dornfontein* was put in dories and left to reach shore on their own. The men arrived safely at Gannet Rock the next day, where Keeper Allen Wilson took them in.

In August of 1930 or 1931, work began on a new keeper's dwelling. Keeper Donald Wilson and his family received word on a Friday that they had to move their belongings out of the house and into the tower by Monday, when a crew would arrive and begin tearing down the old dwelling. Twelve workmen lived in the tower with the keepers until the construction work was finished in November.

During a two-year period starting in 1967, a temporary tower was erected at the station to display a light while the old lantern room and Fresnel lens were removed and a new lantern room and modern beacon were installed. The second-order Fresnel lens is now on display in the Grand Manan Museum.

Gannet Rock's last keeper, Barry S. Bagley, left in April of 1996, and in 2002, the Coast Guard solarized the light. In late 2010, the Canadian Coast Guard determined the deteriorating lighthouse was no longer safe for maintenance crews, which means that once the automated light fails, the lighthouse will remain dark.

3. Southwest Head

John H. Harding, agent of the department of marine for New Brunswick, visited Grand Manan in 1876 and reported that a lighthouse was needed on the island's southwest point. A contract for the lighthouse was awarded in 1878 to Angus W. Fisher, who sent his master builder, B. J. Austin, and seven workmen to the site.

The southern end of Grand Manan Island is known for its precipitous cliffs, and the lighthouse was built atop one of these known as Gull Cliff. The builders incorrectly oriented the structure, running it east-west instead of north-south, which placed a blank panel in the lantern room facing seaward instead of landward.

The first lighting, scheduled for January 1, 1880, had to be postponed until the lantern room was adjusted. The lighthouse, which consisted of a square, wooden tower, measuring 13.1 metres tall, with an attached keeper's dwelling, was finally placed in operation on February 1, 1880. The catoptric light in the lantern room made one revolution every two minutes, producing three white flashes and three red flashes with intervals of eclipse of ten seconds. The total cost for the lighthouse came to $4,164.

Walter B. McLaughlin, who had previously served at Gannet Rock for twenty-six years, was appointed the first keeper at an annual salary of $500. Keeper McLaughlin "found the buildings badly constructed, in fact a perfect sham. The storms beat through in every direction, the shingles and clapboards were nothing better than refuse for lumber. The top of the tower was only covered with one thickness of cotton duck with one coat of paint."

"Into this lighthouse," Keeper McLaughlin later wrote, "I removed my large family during Christmas week, 1879, and…spent the worst winter of my life." The living space had just one sleeping room in the first storey and one room in the upper, half-storey that was supposed to have been partitioned into three rooms. Keeper McLaughlin procured lumber and doors from Saint John to finish the upper storey, and then proceeded to build an

Aerial view of Southwest Head Lighthouse in 2011 with adjacent communication tower.

addition to the dwelling and a large barn. He also cleared and drained the lighthouse lot and built a 3.2-kilometre road to connect the station with the highway road.

Keeper McLaughlin spent $2,820 of his own money for these improvements and even sold land and bonds to do so. Although he wrote several letters to the department of marine asking for reimbursement and sent a photograph showing his improvements, Keeper McLaughlin was never compensated. Rather, the department replied, "if a keeper leaves a station no allowance will be made him for any private buildings nor can he exercise any right of property over such."

After forty-seven years of service, Keeper McLaughlin retired at the age of seventy-two, and his son-in-law, Turner Ingalls, Jr., was appointed keeper in January of 1901.

Keeper Ingalls submitted his letter of resignation on June 17, 1907, and was replaced by Clyde S. Ingersoll on July 10. Ingalls asked one hundred dollars of Keeper Ingersoll for the station's barn that McLaughlin had built and willed to him. Ingersoll complied with the demand, but when he submitted a request for compensation, he was informed that the department already owned the barn.

Original Southwest Head Lighthouse atop Gull Cliff.
(Michel Forand)

Travel Instructions: From North Head on Grand Manan Island, follow Route 776 southwest for 26.1 kilometres.

Established: 1880 (present tower 1959)

Position: 44.60081 N, -66.90550 W

Light: White flash every 10 s

Tower Height: 9.9 metres

Focal Plane: 47.5 metres

Description: White rectangular tower rising from corner of one-storey white building, red lantern.

In 1959, a modern lighthouse was built, and when the work was complete, the old one was torn down. Two new dwellings were built while the lighthouse was under construction, and a third dwelling was added later. Ottawa Benson, who was keeper at Southwest Head during this transition, was the great-grandson of Walter McLaughlin, the first keeper.

During the night of February 26, 1963, Ottawa Benson and his wife, Hildred, heard a thump at their door. Upon opening, Hildred found a man covered with snow who stammered, "Me and my brother's been blown ashore. I got up the bank, but he's still down there." Keeper Benson was dumbfounded. Others had wrecked at the base of the towering cliff before, but no one had ever managed to scale it.

Billy and Floyd Jones had left Haycock Harbor, Maine, the previous morning in a leaky motorboat to gather periwinkles. Their engine failed just as a gale struck, and the two were blown out to sea. After twelve hours of bailing, vomiting, and praying, they ran aground below the blinking light at Southwest Head. The brothers managed to climb to a ledge above the pounding surf, but Floyd, numb with cold, could go no farther. Billy pressed on and managed to reach the lighthouse three hours later. A rescue party of seventeen men, including the bandy-legged Vernon Bagley, was summoned to the scene. The group consensus was to wait until morning as it would be murder to send anyone down the cliff in the dark, but Vern Bagley protested, knowing that Floyd would not survive the night.

With a nylon rope tied securely about their waists,

Vern and assistant keeper Sidney Guptill ventured over the edge of the cliff, but after a short distance, they lost their footing and clambered back to the top in defeat. Dejected and a bit embarrassed, Vern thought for a while then proclaimed, "Yessir, I sure would!" and headed straight back to the cliff.

With renewed determination, Vern Bagley started down the bluff and this time succeeded in locating Floyd, whose clothes were stiff with ice. Wrapping Floyd's arms around his waist and jamming them under the rope, Vern gave three sharp tugs on the rope to initiate the haul-up. Eight metres from the top, Vern's legs gave out, and he was forced to wedge the then-unconscious Floyd behind a boulder and proceed to the top alone. Exhausted from the ninety-minute rescue, Vern collapsed in a snowbank. Sid Guptill then went over the cliff and returned a half hour later with Floyd.

The next day, the Jones brothers tearfully thanked Vern Bagley, who declared the pair to be "tougher'n tripe." A crowd of three hundred later packed the gym at the island's high school to see Vern Bagley receive the Carnegie Silver Medal for heroism and Sid Guptill a bronze medal.

After the ceremony, Vern was asked about his strange announcement of "Yessir, I would!" before he went over the cliff a second time. "Wal," he replied, "I'd been tellin' myself all the reasons why I couldn't go back over that cliff. But then this idea hit me so hard, 'Would you go if it was your own brother?' that I answered out loud. Then I just had to go. 'Cause when you get right down to it, we're all suppose to be brothers."

Southwest Head lost its final keeper with the retirement of Doug Daggett in October 1987.

4. Seal Cove Breakwater

A square, pyramidal tower was placed on the western breakwater at Seal Cove in 1936. The tower measured 4.9 metres tall and displayed a fixed red light from a seventh-order lens. Today, a cylindrical mast displays a flashing green light from a modern breakwater.

Seal Cove Breakwater, 1940. (Canadian Coast Guard)

5. Grand Harbour (Ross Island)

In 1784, Moses Gerrish led a group of fifty Loyalist families to the land on the eastern side of Grand Harbour in 1784 and named it Ross Island, in honour of Thomas Ross, a fellow settler. The resulting village was the first permanent settlement in the Grand Manan Archipelago.

After mariners petitioned the government for a lighthouse to mark Grand Harbour, a contract for $1,050 was awarded in 1878 to Messrs. H. H. Bowie & Co. of Saint John, who hired Charles and George Short, master shipbuilders from St. Andrews, to construct the lighthouse. Fish Fluke Point was purchased from Isaac Newton for $150 as the site for the lighthouse, and work on the structure was pursued during the summer of

Grand Harbour Lighthouse as it appeared in better days before the devastating Groundhog Day Gale. (Library and Archives Canada)

1879. The resulting square, wooden tower, 9.8 metres tall, with an attached keeper's dwelling, first displayed its fixed-white light on October 10.

Henry McLaughlin, the first keeper, had a long history at lighthouses in the area, accepting his first assignment in 1843 to isolated Gannet Rock Lighthouse. He remained there for ten years and then served at Head Harbour before spending four years at Grand Harbour.

Sitting on an exposed point, the lighthouse was often damaged during heavy gales. In 1891 $71.69 was spent to replace protective work and repair injuries sustained during a storm. The following year, $55 was required to replace an abutment that had been carried away by the sea.

Keeper Mark Daggett had been serving for nearly fourteen years when charges of political partisanship, failure to give proper attention to the station, and being absent from the station and unable to assist in a drowning situation were brought against him in 1897. Retaining one's job as a keeper was not easy, as the position was a political appointment and people often trumped up charges to obtain the position for themselves or friends. Keeper Daggett emphatically denied the charges, calling them "false from beginning to end." To refute the third and most serious charge, Daggett

In 1999, there was still a chance to save this lighthouse. By 2009, when this photo was taken, there is little to save.

pointed out that the person who signed the complaint was under a charge of felony.

In his defense, Keeper Daggett presented a petition signed by fifty-two members of the community certifying "his strict attention to his duties as a lightkeeper and as being a man who always minds his own business in all matters." Daggett retained his position until his passing in February of 1900. His widow, Mary, petitioned for her son, who had been serving as an assistant, to be appointed keeper until the family could pay off the medical expenses incurred during her husband's protracted illness. It seems politics trumped charity, as Mary Daggett was given the customary gratuity of two months' salary, and the position was awarded to another.

Harry McDowell was the longest-serving keeper at Grand Harbour Lighthouse. He and his wife, Sadie, arrived in 1914 and left in 1948, after raising nine children at the lighthouse. The couple had three children before moving to Ross Island, but the other six were born at the lighthouse. The McDowell children had many happy memories of growing up at the lighthouse, but having to walk to Grand Harbour to attend school might not have been among them.

After a light was placed on Ingalls Head Breakwater, Grand Harbour Lighthouse was discontinued on August 1, 1963. A powerful storm on February 2, 1976, known

Travel Instructions: From Route 776 at Grand Harbour, take Thoroughfare Road to its end and park. At low tide, Ross Island is accessible by foot or with a 4x4 vehicle. From the end of Thoroughfare Road, it is 2.4 kilometres to the lighthouse. The lighthouse can also be viewed from Ingalls Head.

Established: 1879

Position: 44.66688 N, -66.74915 W

Light: Inactive since 1963

Tower Height: 9.8 metres

Focal Plane: 12.2 metres

Description: White pyramidal tower, with red lantern and attached dwelling

as the Groundhog Day Gale, just happened to coincide with abnormally high tides. The storm wreaked havoc on coastal communities in southern New Brunswick, and the abandoned lighthouse received significant damage.

In May 1999, *Lighthouse Digest* declared Grand Harbour Lighthouse to be "North America's Most Endangered Lighthouse" and launched a fundraising campaign to save the structure. Errol Rainess, who lived in New York and had purchased Ross Island, sight unseen, in 1984, agreed to match any funds that could be raised in sixty days. Ten thousand dollars was reportedly collected through the effort, but after Rainess received a cheque for that amount, he eluded further contact.

It appears there is little hope for Grand Harbour Lighthouse, which continues its gradual descent into total ruin.

6. Long Point

Long Point Lighthouse, 2011.

Travel Instructions: To reach White Head Island, take the free thirty-minute ferry from Ingalls Head on Grand Manan. Once on White Head Island, turn right, proceed 0.5 kilometres, and then turn left onto Long Point Road. After another 0.5 kilometres, you may need to park and walk the last kilometre to the lighthouse depending on road conditions.

Established: 1929 (present structure 1966)

Position: 44.61367 N, -66.70964 W

Light: White, on 6 s, off 6 s

Tower Height: 11.4 metres

Focal Plane: 15.6 metres

Description: White rectangular tower rising from corner of one-storey white building, red lantern

With a population of roughly two hundred, White Head Island is the only other inhabited island in the Grand Manan Archipelago besides Grand Manan Island. Samuel de Champlain sought shelter at White Head Island during a storm in October 1606, but permanent settlers would not arrive for another two hundred years.

In October 1927, a petition calling for the establishment of a fog alarm at Long Point, the southernmost point of White Head Island, was sent to the department of marine by 330 residents of Grand Manan and Nova Scotia. At that time, roughly 125 fishing boats operated off the island.

In September 1928, tenders were invited for constructing a combined dwelling and fog alarm building, but before a contract was signed, the district engineer declared the design unacceptable, as a keeper living in a similar structure was nearly asphyxiated by fumes from a fog alarm. Besides, a vibrating and noisy fog alarm didn't make the best housemate.

New tenders were invited in March 1929 for three separate structures: a fog alarm building, a dwelling, and a boathouse. Five bids were submitted, and the lowest bid of $7,489 by G. Stephen Whitehead was accepted.

The fog signal equipment supplied to the station consisted of two three-horsepower engine/compressor units, furnished by the Fairbanks Morse Company, air and oil tanks, and a diaphone. Arthur Wilson was the first keeper of the fog alarm and served at the station for nearly thirty years.

A combination lighthouse and fog alarm building was built at Long Point in 1966. Shortly thereafter, the whistle house was torn down and the old keeper's dwelling was burned, requiring subsequent keepers to provide their own accommodations.

7. Gull Cove

The 1910 Gull Cove Lighthouse seen here in 1935 with the mast light it replaced. (Canadian Coast Guard)

A light, consisting of a lantern hoisted atop a 10.7-metre-tall mast, was established at Gull Cove on December 30, 1902, to serve as a guide for fishing boats. The mast stood 183 metres back from the shore near the home of Lewis Frankland, who first tended the light.

In 1910, a square, pyramidal, 14.9-metre-tall wooden tower, built under contract by Edward Rourke for $1,220, replaced the pole light. This tower employed a fourth-order lens to produce a fixed white light. The lighthouse was discontinued in 1981, relocated to private property, and later torn down.

8. Great Duck Island

Great Duck fog alarm and dwelling, 1901. (Library and Archives Canada)

Great Duck Island is located 3.4 kilometres off the eastern shore of Grand Manan near Woodward's Cove, and companions Low Duck Island and High Duck Island lie just to the north.

In the early 1880s, a petition signed by over two-thirds of the inhabitants of Grand Manan was sent to Ottawa calling for the establishment of a steam fog whistle on Great Duck Island, then commonly known as Big Duck Island. Parliament responded in 1884 with an appropriation, and a $2,070 contract was awarded to G. S. Mayes. A T-shaped building was erected on the island to house the fog alarm equipment, and a small keeper's dwelling and boathouse were built nearby.

Samuel G. Dinsmore was appointed the first engineer, and the fog alarm was put into operation on October 1, 1886, sounding six-second blasts followed by thirty-five seconds of silence. A report in 1887 noted that the fog alarm was "giving great satisfaction to the fishermen and vessels coasting around the south and east sides of the island."

Due to acid in the water, the tubes in the fog alarm's boiler used to heat the water had to be replaced about every four months. A second boiler, made by Messrs. Carrier, Laine, & Co. at a cost of $1,386, joined the old boiler at the station in June of 1896.

Great Duck Island Lighthouse with salmon farm in background, 2011.

Travel Instructions: The lighthouse is best viewed by boat, but a distant view is possible from Grand Manan.

Established: 1886 (present structure 1966)

Position: 44.68431 N, -66.69286 W

Light: White, on 1 s, eclipse 9 s

Tower Height: 8.9 metres

Focal Plane: 15.3 metres

Description: White rectangular tower, red lantern

In 1915, the steam plant was converted to oil, and a Class "B" diaphone fog alarm was installed under the direction of F. J. Lewis for $2,469. The station lost its boathouse to fire on February 25, 1926, and the keeper's dwelling burned down on October 5, 1955, due to a defective chimney. Two replacement dwellings were soon added to the station, and in 1966 a combination lighthouse and fog alarm building was constructed. The station was automated in 1984, and in 2008 the fog alarm building was demolished.

9. Swallowtail

Swallowtail Lighthouse, which overlooks the entrance to North Head Harbour, welcomes all travellers arriving at Grand Manan by ferry, but few know the amazing history of this beacon or appreciate the hardships endured by its keepers.

The 1,009-ton, three-masted *Lord Ashburton* was en route to Saint John when it foundered on the northern shore of Grand Manan during a gale on January 19, 1857. James Lawson, a member of the crew, scaled a nearby rocky headland, now named Ashburton Head, and stumbled a kilometre to Long Eddy, where he collapsed in a hay barn. He was discovered the next morning by James Tatton, who later became keeper at Long Eddy, and a rescue was launched that saved seven badly frozen members of the crew of twenty-nine. A memorial to the *Lord Ashburton* seamen stands in the Anglican Church cemetery at North Head. James Lawson had both his feet partially amputated, but after recuperating in Saint John, he returned to Grand Manan, married an islander, and worked as a shoemaker.

The Ashburton disaster highlighted the need for a navigational aid in the area, and just months later the House of Assembly recommended that a light be erected on "the Northern Head of Grand Manan."

Plans and specifications for the lighthouse and a dwelling were drawn up in 1859, and a £495 contract was awarded to John P. McKay of Saint John. Mr. McKay and I. Woodward, superintendent of lighthouses in the Bay of Fundy, left Saint John on June

A freshly painted Swallowtail Lighthouse, 2009.

27, 1859, and proceeded to Grand Manan, where they selected a spot for the contemplated buildings on "the Swallow's Tail."

John McKay then proceeded to construct the octagonal lighthouse and dwelling that year, but due to a delay in receiving the lantern room, the inaugural lighting didn't occur until July 7, 1860. The lighthouse initially employed nine lamps and reflectors to cover three-quarters of a circle, but an additional lamp and reflector were later added to benefit vessels going to the

Travel Instructions: From the ferry terminal road on Grand Manan Island, turn right onto Pettes Cove Road and then take the first left onto Old Airport Road. After 0.3 kilometres, turn right onto Lighthouse Road, continue 0.5 kilometres, and park near the boathouse. A short, steep hike is required to reach the lighthouse, which can also be viewed from the ferry.

Established: 1860

Position: 44.76419 N, -66.73269 W

Light: White, on 4 s, eclipse 2 s

Tower Height: 16.2 metres

Focal Plane: 37.1 metres

Description: White octagonal tower, red lantern

western part of Long Island Bay. A bridge to connect the headland to the point on which the lighthouse stood was constructed in 1861.

Swallowtail Lighthouse was in first-rate order when the Saxby Gale struck on October 4, 1869. The hurricane, accompanied by an unusually high tide, created a two-metre surge that caused significant damage in the Bay of Fundy. The station's boat was destroyed, and a large portion of the landing slip washed away. The keeper's dwelling was so shaken by the storm that two chains were strung over the roof and secured to the rock on each side to keep it in position. The foundation of the lighthouse was significantly damaged, necessitating the construction of a substantial stone wall beneath the tower.

Jonathan Kent, the light's first keeper, retired in 1873 and was replaced by his son, John W. Kent. Keeper John W. Kent regularly received praise in the department of marine reports, including this example from 1877:

Everything at this Station is in first class condition, and Mr. Kent takes great pride in keeping this Station, and its appurtenances in good order. He is a man of good

taste, and this Station is visited by great numbers of strangers and excursionists who come to the Island during the summer season.

Mr. Kent had given the lighthouse a coat of paint, which had lightened it up and greatly improved its appearance. Altogether, this Station may be considered the model station of the Department.

In 1907, a fourth-order French lens was installed in the lantern room along with a Chance vapour installation, and the light's signature was changed to occulting white.

G. N. Breen constructed a wooden fog bell tower in 1914 at a cost of $974. This structure was moved in 1920 from the extreme tip of the peninsula to a spot adjacent to the tower, where it could be more readily serviced.

Tragedy struck Swallowtail Lighthouse in August 1936 when Elodie Foster was tending the light while her husband was visiting Southwest Head Lighthouse. While igniting the light's alcohol burner that night, Elodie's clothes caught on fire. She rushed down the tower's stairs and exited the lighthouse. Her son Leonard and two daughters came to her aid. Leonard raced up the tower and extinguished the flames in the lantern room before the fire spread to the wooden tower. Elodie managed to survive the night but passed away the next day from her burns.

A new dwelling was constructed for the lighthouse keeper in 1958, and the old one was torn down. Keeper Grimmer Ingersoll, who served from 1960 until the lighthouse was de-staffed in 1986, witnessed many changes at the station. Not long after arriving, he moved the old boathouse from Grand Harbour Lighthouse to a spot up the hill from the station. In the 1960s the Coast Guard removed the beautiful twelve-over-eight windows that adorned the sides of the lighthouse to reduce maintenance. In 1980, the station's fog bell was relocated to the Grand Manan Museum, but it was returned to the station in 2011.

Ownership of the lighthouse property was transferred to the Village of North Head in 1994 and then to the village of Grand Manan in 1996, when the island's villages were amalgamated.

The horror film *Hemoglobin* was filmed at the lighthouse in 1996, and soon thereafter the dwelling opened as the Swallowtail Inn, a bed and breakfast run by Catherine Neves and her sister Crystal Cook. After operating for nearly a decade, the inn was shuttered in 2004.

In March 2008, the village council announced that the keeper's dwelling would be sold as repairs had cost the community eighty thousand dollars. A well-publicized meeting was held on April 4 to generate ideas for saving the dwelling and resulted in the creation of the Swallowtail Keepers Society, whose mission is to rejuvenate the station and make it a symbol of civic pride. The village council, a bit surprised by the islanders' passion, quickly rescinded their motion to sell the dwelling, and on November 2, 2009, the village of Grand Manan signed a twenty-year lease with the society.

The Swallowtail Keepers Society organized a celebration at the lighthouse on July 7, 2010, 150 years to the day since the beacon was first activated. Laurel Hinsdale, daughter of Keeper Grimmer Ingersoll, was on hand to

Swallowtail Lighthouse with fog bell and full complement of outbuildings. (Canadian Coast Guard)

share her memories of living at Swallowtail. She recalled being blown off her feet while holding her mother's hand and having to crawl across a wooden bridge with her father to reach the safety of the keeper's dwelling during the Groundhog Gale in 1976.

Thanks to the efforts of the society, Swallowtail Lighthouse will continue to be a place where memories are made.

10. *Long Eddy Point (Grand Manan)*

On May 1, 1874, the following Notice to Mariners was issued:

> *Notice is hereby given, that a steam fog-whistle has been erected on the north-west head of Grand Manan, in the Bay of Fundy—latitude 44 47 9 N., longitude 66 45 7 W.*
>
> *The whistle is erected on the extreme north-west head of the island, and is elevated 80 feet above high water. In thick weather, fogs and snowstorms, it will be sounded, so as to give three blasts of four seconds duration in each minute, with an interval of sixteen seconds between each blast.*

Fog alarm on beach at Long Eddy Point. (Library and Archives Canada)

Looking out from Long Eddy Point Lighthouse toward Campobello Island and Maine.

Travel Instructions: From the ferry landing in North Head, turn left, drive 1.5 kilometres, and then turn right onto Whistle Road. Continue for 5 kilometres to the lighthouse.

Established: 1874 (present structure 1966)

Position: 44.79928 N, -66.78522 W

Light: Red flash every 8 s

Tower Height: 9.3 metres

Focal Plane: 38.3 metres

Description: White rectangular tower rising from corner of one-storey white building, red lantern

A sum of $8,318.43 was spent in constructing the steam fog whistle, whose activation was delayed due to the destruction by fire of the Allan Brothers foundry in Carleton. The firm received an extension, and the fog signal, which could frequently be heard in Eastport, finally commenced operation on July 1, 1874. James Tatton, who owned the land on which the fog alarm was built, was appointed the station's first engineer at an annual salary of $700.

A steamer delivered the station's supplies to a wharf connected to the station by a good wagon road. The 1875 department of marine report noted, "An addition to Mr. Tatton's, the keeper's dwelling-house, is very much needed, to accommodate the assistant engineer's family. The house was only built for one small family, and there are now two families living in it. Were it not that the assistant is a son of Mr. Tatton it might be impossible for the two families to get along together. The assistant has a wife and two children." A lean-to shed was soon added to the south side of the dwelling to house the assistant keeper and his family.

The fog alarm building was built on a terrace, halfway up the cliff, and was situated atop water tanks needed to run the steam engine that powered Long Eddy's steam whistle, known locally as "The Whistle." A covered passageway connected the fog alarm building to a nearby coal shed, which was fed by a wooden chute that reached the top of the hill.

After thirty years of use, the original fog alarm building required extensive repairs, and the marine department opted to build a new structure on the beach at the foot of the cliff, where the sound could be better directed seaward. The new foghorn was put into operation on January 15, 1905.

A new keeper's dwelling was constructed at Long Eddy in 1948 at a cost of $13,627. After Long Eddy had been operating solely as a fog alarm station for nearly a century, a combination lighthouse and fog alarm building was built atop the bluff at the northern end of the island in 1966.

11. Southwest (Southern) Wolf Island

In 1853, thirty inhabitants of St. Andrews petitioned the House of Assembly calling for a lighthouse on White Horse Island, located off the northern tip of Campobello Island. The commissioners of lighthouses for the Bay of Fundy concluded that a light on Southern Wolf Island or the northern head of Grand Manan would be of greater benefit and directed one to be built if the cost could be covered by the lighthouse fund.

While visiting Saint John in 1853, Commander Shortland of the surveying steamer HMS *Columbia* was requested to determine the most suitable spot for a lighthouse on the Wolves, a collection of five islands. Circumstances beyond his control prevented the commander from fulfilling the request, and no further action was taken on the matter until Confederation. In 1870, John Harley, inspector of lights in New Brunswick, recommended that a light "on the southern one of the group of Wolve's [sic] Islands…would prove of great service."

A lighthouse was constructed on Southern Wolf Island in 1871, and Keeper William Cline, who received an annual salary of five hundred dollars, displayed its light for the first time on November 20 of that year.

Original Southwest Wolf Lighthouse. (Library and Archives Canada)

This Southwest Wolf Island lighthouse tower, seen here in 1976, was used from 1962 to 1982. (Canadian Coast Guard)

Travel Instructions: Southwest Wolf Island is visible at a distance from the Grand Manan ferry halfway through the voyage.

Established: 1871 (present tower 1982)

Position: 44.93661 N, -66.73319 W

Light: White, on 1 s, eclipse 9 s

Tower Height: 11.4 metres

Focal Plane: 38.1 metres

Description: White cylindrical tower, red lantern

The revolving light had two faces, each containing three lamps set in reflectors, and produced a white flash every ninety seconds. The lighthouse consisted of a square wooden keeper's dwelling with a square tower rising from its hipped roof.

In the fall of 1873, Keeper Snell hired three men, whom he paid $1.50 per day plus board for a period of thirty-six days, to build a breakwater and wharf on the western side of the island. After completing the work, Snell sent a letter to the marine agent in Saint John, along with a bill for the labour and material:

> *Now, Sir, in further explanation, I would say that these works were undertaken by me without direct instruction from the Department I admit, but clearly and solely in the interest of the Department and as being of vital importance and necessity for the better protection and safety of the property of the Department placed in this extremely isolated and dangerous part.*
>
> *I trust then that the Department will see how useful, how efficacious they are for the purpose intended, and will consider that I, in my zeal and my desire to promote the interest of the Department, have but anticipated their wishes in this respect, and in all fairness and justice, will reimburse me for my outlay in its behalf.*

The marine agent recommended that Keeper Snell be reimbursed the $331 he had spent for material and

Aerial view of Southwest Wolf Island Lighthouse in 2011 with a fishing wier in the foreground.

labour, as the work had "proved of great service and convenience to the department."

In 1905, a third-order lens, illuminated by petroleum vapour burned under an incandescent mantle, was installed in the lantern room to produce a bright, white flash every five seconds.

A skeletal tower replaced the original 1871 lighthouse in 1962. The present fibreglass tower dates from 1982.

12. *Mulholland Point*

In 1882, Parliament provided funds for a lighthouse near the southern end of Campobello Island to guide vessels through Lubec Narrows, the small passage separating the island from the United States mainland. After the exact site was selected and specifications prepared, tenders were invited for the work, and a $790 contract was awarded to Angus Fisher of St. George in 1883.

Mulholland Point Lighthouse was completed in 1884, but its fixed white light was not exhibited until 1885. E. Chanteloup, a Montreal establishment that outfitted many Canadian lighthouses, supplied the lantern and lighting apparatus at a cost of $683.26, and Malachi Parker was hired as the first keeper.

Around the time Mulholland Lighthouse was

Travel Instructions: From Lubec, Maine, take the F.D.R. Memorial Bridge over Lubec Narrows, passing through the customs station, and take your first left to reach the lighthouse.

Established: 1885

Position: 44.86313 N, -66.97967 W

Light: Inactive since 1963

Tower Height: 13.4 metres

Focal Plane: 18.3 metres

Description: White octagonal tower, red lantern

Mulholland Point Lighthouse overlooks a narrow channel that runs between Campobello Island and Lubec, Maine.

constructed, Campobello Island was becoming a popular summer colony for wealthy Canadians and Americans. Among these was James Roosevelt Sr., whose wife, Sara Delano, had a number of cousins living in Maine. The Roosevelt family made Campobello Island their summer home starting in 1883, and it was there that their son Franklin Delano Roosevelt, who became the thirty-second president of the United States, spent his summers.

In 1903, Franklin brought his future wife, Eleanor, to the family's summer cottage. After the couple married in 1905, the nearby Kuhn Cottage became their own Campobello Island retreat.

Franklin D. Roosevelt served as assistant secretary of the Navy from 1913 to 1920, during which time he made an inspection to Maine aboard the USS *Flusser*. Taking the helm, the future president captained the vessel through Lubec Narrows, earning the respect of an initially concerned Lieutenant William F. "Bull" Halsey. Halsey later wrote, "As Mr. Roosevelt made his first turn, I saw him look aft and check the swing of our stern. My worries were over; he knew his business."

At his island cottage in 1921, Franklin fell ill with a paralytic illness, which resulted in total and permanent paralysis from his waist down. After suffering this affliction, Roosevelt did not return to Campobello Island until 1933, the year he began serving as president.

Eleanor returned to the island more frequently,

bringing along their children and close friends. She enjoyed the solitude found on Campobello, which had no telephones at the time, and even found solace in the fog that frequently shrouds the island in the summer. "Fog is nice if you know a place and are with someone you like," she wrote. "It is like a winter storm. It shuts you in and gives you a close and intimate feeling and adds to the joy of your fire."

A few weeks before her passing in 1962, Eleanor Roosevelt made her last trip to Campobello Island to attend the dedication of the Franklin Delano Roosevelt Memorial Bridge that linked the island to the mainland. The navigational lights on the new bridge made Mulholland Lighthouse unnecessary, and it was decommissioned in 1963.

The tower and adjacent shed were sold to Clifford Calder in 1963. The Look family, who owned an adjacent lobster pound, later purchased the lighthouse from Mr. Calder. On December 4, 1984, brothers Austin, Lynn, Anthony, Shirley, and Donald Look donated the lighthouse to Roosevelt Campobello International Park in memory of Clifford Calder.

13. Head Harbour (East Quoddy)

In February 1829, the House of Assembly of New Brunswick appropriated £400 for "defraying the expense of building a Light House on the northern head of Campo Bello Island." Work on Head Harbour Lighthouse soon commenced, and the light was placed in operation later that year with John Snell as its first keeper. The total expense for constructing the lighthouse, the wooden octagonal tower that remains standing today, was £656. The importance of this lighthouse is illustrated by it being the first constructed in New Brunswick outside Saint John Harbour. West Quoddy Lighthouse was established nearby in the United States in 1808, and Head Harbour Lighthouse is sometimes called East Quoddy Lighthouse to differentiate the two.

Head Harbour Lighthouse was built on a small, rocky islet, located just off the northern tip of Campobello Island and accessible by land only around low tide. Access to the lighthouse was primarily by boat until £80 was expended in 1830 to establish a road between the northern end of the island and Wilson's Beach, the nearest settlement.

The April 10, 1830, edition of the *Courier* in Saint John recorded that during a gale the sea broke nearly half-way up the lighthouse and carried away Keeper Snell's boat, firewood, spring water, barn, cow, and every other removable article. Through "her own instinct or sagacity," the cow managed to reach the shore of a neighbouring island.

Keeper Snell resided in the lower portion of the lighthouse until a dwelling was erected near the tower in 1840. At that time, eight lamps set in twenty-two-inch reflectors were used in the lantern room, which was considered too small, as the keeper was unable to clean the lamps and reflectors without significant inconvenience.

In 1842, a larger lantern room was placed atop the tower, and the original lantern room was installed on St. Andrews Lighthouse. That same year, a large red cross was painted on the eastern side of Head Harbour's white tower to provide a distinctive daymark.

Mary Snell grew up at Head Harbour Lighthouse, where she lost her sight at the age of seven due to an illness. In her later years, she recorded memories of her childhood. "It would seem as though I instinctively felt that I would not always enjoy the blessing of sight, and eagerly sought to satisfy my soul with long and earnest gazing on the beauty and grandeur of creation." Once blind, she had to rely on her hearing to experience life at the lighthouse:

At times, when in a listless mood, if the weather was pleasant, I would go out of doors and sit down in some spot where I could listen to any sound there might be to listen to. The usual sounds were the screaming of the sea gulls as they darted hither and thither, skimming the water in quest of food; the splashing of the wheels of a passing steamboat; the voices of the fishermen talking as they passed and repassed in their fishing boats, with now and then the spouting of a whale, for these great fish frequently make their appearance in the bay, often swimming along within a few yards of the shore. Sometimes the only sound to be heard was the lowing of the cattle, the bleating of sheep, or the barking of dogs on the neighbouring Island. That which pleased and interested me most was the singing of the sailors while getting their vessels underway preparatory to leaving the harbor, to the entrance of which the lighthouse is a faithful guide to the mariner by night in all seasons of the year. When a dozen or more sailors unite in singing, as they usually do when weighing anchor, their concert is well worth hearing.

In 1874, mammoth flat-wick burners were substituted for the small half-inch flat-wick burners previously used. The resulting improvement in the light was noted in a letter by E. B. Winchester, captain of the International Steamship Company's vessel *New York*, to John H. Harding, the marine agent in Saint John.

Head Harbour Lighthouse, 1902. (Canadian Coast Guard)

View of Head Harbour Lighthouse at half tide from a whale-watching boat.

I have great pleasure in informing you that [due to] the increased number of lights, together with the very marked improvements which have been made by increasing the power of the old lights in the Bay of Fundy…the mariner is now able to navigate the bay during thick and foggy weather with much less risk of life and property than previous to these valuable guides, which I find are well attended, and can be reckoned on with great safety. While on this subject, I would wish to call the attention of your prompt and energetic Minister to a want that has long been required and has been the subject of frequent discussion by the International Steamship Company, as well as mariners generally trading on the coast near the entrance of Passamaquoddy Bay, Viz.: the necessity of a steam fog-whistle at Head Harbour Light-house.

In 1875, Gannet Rock Lighthouse received a new signal gun, and its old gun was shipped to Head Harbour, where a safer one was needed. Steps were taken in 1877 to establish a new steam-powered Neptune fog trumpet on the east side of the dwelling, and it commenced operation in October of that year. The horn, which cost $2,500, did not function satisfactorily, and it was discontinued the following year. A new trumpet of an "improved description" was put in operation on January 30, 1880, and was hailed as "the loudest and best sounding fog-alarm in the Bay of Fundy." As the station now required two men to operate it, Angus Fisher was awarded a $1,100 contract in 1885 to construct a new dwelling for the fog alarm engineer.

In 1887, a new iron lantern room with large plate glass windows was installed atop the tower to house a third-order lens, and an addition was made to the engineer's dwelling. A new fog alarm building was constructed in 1915 and outfitted with a class "C" diaphone fog signal.

Coast Guard personnel staffed Head Harbour Lighthouse until 1986. In 1988, the original 1829 tower, the oldest surviving lighthouse in New Brunswick, received classified status from the Federal Heritage Building Review Office. The Friends of the Head Harbour Lightstation was formed in 2000 to preserve, protect, and promote the unique heritage of the lighthouse.

Travel Instructions: From Lubec, Maine, take the F. D. R. Memorial Bridge onto Campobello Island and follow NB Route 774 to the northern end of the island. After 4 kilometres, you will need to turn right to remain on NB Route 774, and from this point it is 11.5 kilometres to the northern tip of the island. Access to the islet on which the lighthouse is located is only possible for a few hours around low tide. The tower and dwelling can be toured during the summer for a fee.

Established: 1829

Position: 44.95794 N, -66.90006 W

Light: Fixed red

Tower Height: 15.5 metres

Focal Plane: 17.6 metres

Description: White octagonal tower, with red cross and red lantern

14. Cherry Island

Modern Cherry Island Light with its prominent solar panels.

On June 16, 1903, a fog bell was established on Cherry Island to help mariners enter the St. Croix River. The bell was surmounted by a square, wooden tower that stood 5.2 metres tall. During foggy weather, machinery would strike the bell two times in quick succession every six seconds. The machinery cost $400, and John Kelly, superintendent of lights, constructed the tower for $633.34.

Harvey V. Chaffey was responsible for the station from 1903 until 1914, when Mendel Fountain took charge. The original bell was used until 1914, when a "better fog bell" was installed under the direction of D. J. Gallagher at an expense of $157.62. A No. 4 Gamewell striking mechanism was placed in operation in 1920.

In 1969, a directional light was placed atop the truncated fog tower, which was later replaced by the current cylindrical tower.

Cherry Island Fog Bell, 1935. (Canadian Coast Guard)

Travel Instructions: A distant view of the light is possible from the Campobello-Deer Island Ferry.

Established: 1903

Position: 44.91867 N, -66.96667 W

Light: White, on 0.5 s, eclipse 4.5 s

Tower Height: 7.5 metres

Focal Plane: 9.8 metres

Description: White cylindrical tower, with red and white horizontal bands

15. Leonardville

In 1913, A. L. Mury erected Leonardville Lighthouse atop a cliff on the eastern shore of Deer Island for $896. The lighthouse, which originally employed a sixth-order dioptric lens to send forth a white light, marked the western side of the entrance to Leonardville Harbour, a very small and shallow bay located between Deer Island and Bar Island, a small island just offshore.

Alonzo H. Conley was the first keeper of the lighthouse, and in 1936 he wrote to his superior, J. C. Chesley, to tell him of a large meteor that fell into the ocean off Harbour-de-Lute on Campobello Island. Keeper Conley was informed of this unusual event by a resident of that place who reported, "When it struck, the water steamed and hissed like a cauldron of boiling water and bubbled vigorously—large waves washed ashore." Mr. Chesley replied that he would provide the information to the dominion's meteorological department in Toronto.

The best view of Leonardville Lighthouse is from the water.

Travel Instructions: Ferries from L'Etete, Eastport, and Campobello Island service Deer Island. Once on the island, the lighthouse can be seen through the trees from NB Route 172/772 on the eastern side of the island, just south of Leonardville.

Established: 1913

Position: 44.96822 N, -66.95511 W

Light: Fixed white

Tower Height: 8.5 metres

Focal Plane: 20 metres

Description: White pyramidal tower, red-roofed lantern

Mark Point Lighthouse, 1926. (Canadian Coast Guard)

PASSAMAQUODDY BAY
AND
ST. CROIX RIVER

16. *Spruce Point*
17. *Mark Point*

Beacon lights, constructed on the St. Croix River at Mark Point and Spruce Point in 1875, commenced operation on April 1, 1876. The two open-framework towers were twins, measuring 8.5 metres from base to vane and displaying a fixed white light. John Boyd was appointed the first keeper at Spruce Point, while oversight of Mark Point's tower was initially given to Absalom Christie.

The evening of October 8, 1882, was dark and stormy. Keeper John Boyd was away from Spruce Point, leaving the light in the care of his wife, Kate, and daughter, Bertha (Bertie). Kate and Bertie were sitting in their home when they heard anxious cries for help from two men who had been thrown from their capsized sailboat into the swirling, frigid waters of the St. Croix River. Instinctively, Bertie sprang into action, running down to the river and launching the station's boat.

Original Spruce Point Lighthouse. (Canadian Coast Guard)

Rowing out into the river, she soon found the two men desperately clinging to their overturned craft. Bertie quickly assisted the younger gentleman into her rowboat, but it took a mighty effort to free the older, heavier man, who was entangled in the rigging, and pull him aboard.

In recognition of her heroic feat, Bertie was presented a gold watch by the government of Canada and an accompanying chain by the town of St. Stephen. The watch was inscribed "in recognition of her humane exertions in saving life in the St. Croix River." The department of marine honoured her efforts with the gift of a new rowboat, bearing the words "Roberta Grace Boyd, Grace Darling of the Saint Croix" on its stern. Bertie remained humble despite all the attention, saying,

"Please don't speak of it. Indeed, I did nothing worth describing."

Bertie eventually became the official keeper of the light after her father passed away in 1892 "from the effects of a bruise accidentally inflicted while at work with a drawing knife."

Red and white cylindrical towers replaced the wooden towers in 1973 and served until the lights were discontinued in 2001.

18. St. Andrews (Pendlebury)

Constructed in 1833, St. Andrews Lighthouse is the oldest remaining mainland lighthouse in New Brunswick and is commonly referred to as Pendlebury Lighthouse after the family who tended the light for almost one hundred years.

Located at the tip of a peninsula in Passamaquoddy Bay, St. Andrews was founded in 1783 by Loyalists and was an important seaport in the early days of the colony of New Brunswick. Duties were levied on vessels calling at New Brunswick ports to help support the construction and maintenance of lighthouses. In 1832, £784 was collected at St. Andrews, and from the resulting lighthouse fund, £196 was spent in 1833 for "erecting a Light House on Indian Point, at the Eastern entrance of Saint Andrews Harbour." A keeper's dwelling was built the following year.

The deficiencies of St. Andrews Lighthouse, which consisted of a wooden, octagonal tower topped by a lantern room, were noted soon after it was built. The interior of the tower was left unfinished, providing little insulation in the winter, and its original lantern was deemed "utterly unfit." The four lamps set in fifteen-inch reflectors used in the small lantern room left little space for the keeper to manoeuvre while tending the light. The tower was also inadequately secured to the wharf, and shaking the railing atop the lighthouse caused the whole tower to totter.

St. Andrews Lighthouse with nearby wharves. (Michel Forand)

The foundation of the lighthouse was properly secured in 1840, and in 1841, the lantern from Head Harbour was placed atop St. Andrews Lighthouse, making it easier for the keeper to clean and trim the lamps. Seal oil was typically burned in the lamps, but more expensive porpoise oil had to be used during the colder months. In 1857, the light's lamps consumed 179 gallons of seal oil and 32 gallons of porpoise oil.

James Smith, the first keeper, served for nearly a decade until repeated acts of misconduct led to his removal in 1842. The commissioners of lighthouses at Saint Andrews gave the following explanation for his termination: "...his confirmed habits of intoxication left us no course to pursue, and we are assured that

St. Andrews Lighthouse shown badly damaged after part of the seawall collapsed, 1962. (Canadian Coast Guard)

Your Excellency will unite with us in opinion, that the principal qualification of a Keeper ought to be sobriety, for without it there can be no dependence or security, especially in the night when he is concealed from the public eye."

When John Pendlebury transferred from Machias Seal Island Lighthouse in 1842 to become keeper at St. Andrews, he began a family dynasty that continued until Emma Pendlebury, who had been serving as keeper for twenty-one years, resigned when the light was decommissioned in 1938.

The Pendlebury Lighthouse, shortly after having its beautiful new replicated lantern installed, November 2011.

Travel Instructions: Take Highway 127 to St. Andrews and continue through town on Parr Street until it ends, then turn right onto Augustus Street. From Augustus Street, turn right on Patrick Street and continue to the end where there is limited parking near the lighthouse.

Established: 1833

Position: 45.06844 N, -67.04780 W

Light: Inactive since 1938

Tower Height: 6.7 metres

Description: White octagonal tower, red and black lantern

St. Andrews Lighthouse and the adjoining keeper's house were built atop a wharf exposed to the buffeting of the sea. The Saxby Gale of 1869 carried away part of the foundation block, necessitating immediate repairs to the wharf. A heavy gale on November 23, 1874, blew the tower over, but it sustained no serious injury and was righted and moved to the public wharf, where the marine department had to pay rent. After the old lighthouse block was repaired and raised, the tower was returned to its previous location in 1875.

St. Andrews Lighthouse served as a club room for the St. Andrews Yacht Club from its deactivation in 1938 until the outbreak of the Second World War. A portion of the seawall collapsed in the early 1960s imparting a dramatic tilt to the lighthouse. Prompted by an appeal from the Charlotte County Historical Society, the owner of the lighthouse, Ralph Conley, shored up the foundation. Conley owned a processing plant in St. Andrews and ran a restaurant that used the keeper's cottage as an anteroom to promote his product.

Bob Estes, the final owner of Lighthouse Restaurant, transferred ownership of the tower to St. Andrews Civic Trust in 2002, and Godin Ventures moved the tower off the rapidly deteriorating wharf that summer.

In 2003 the deteriorated lantern room, which had been boarded up for years, was removed. When Bob Estes sold Lighthouse Restaurant in 2005, he gave the keeper's cottage and the land under it to the civic trust, which disassembled the structure and placed it in storage.

When Sand Reef Lighthouse was built offshore in 1876, it seems thought was given to discontinuing St. Andrews Lighthouse as that year's *Annual Report of the Department of Marine* included the following: "The inhabitants of St. Andrews still cling to the old buildings and appear unwilling to let them go." This same affection for "old buildings" has driven the current residents of St. Andrews to complete a thorough restoration of the lighthouse and make it once again the focal point of the town's waterfront.

In 2010, the seawall protecting the lighthouse site was completely rebuilt, and St. Andrews Lighthouse was restored and returned to its original location. To cap off the project, a newly fabricated lantern room was placed atop the tower on October 24, 2011.

19. Navy Bar

Built on a shoal extending from Navy Island to mark a dangerous turn into the port of St. Andrews, Navy Bar Lighthouse first displayed its fixed white light on October 17, 1904. The white, rectangular dwelling, with a red octagonal iron lantern centred on its hipped roof, originally stood atop a steel pile foundation, but when the piles were seriously injured by ice, the lighthouse was placed on a rectangular wooden cribwork in 1905. A fog bell and iron boat davits were added to the station in 1907.

C. L. McKeen built the lighthouse under a $2,025 contract, while Messrs. Gould, Shapley & Muir provided the steelwork for the foundation for $2,071.

The Canadian Coast Guard burned down Navy Bar Lighthouse in 1967. Some feel the removal of the lighthouse was in preparation for the Queen Mother's visit to St. Andrews that year, as the structure was considered an eyesore.

Navy Bar Lighthouse at low tide, 1934. (Canadian Coast Guard)

20. Tongue Shoal (Sand Reef)

Activated on January 1, 1876, Sand Reef Lighthouse was built atop a pier on dangerous Tongue Shoal to serve as a guide to all ports in inner Passamaquoddy Bay. Angus Fisher employed a crew of men to construct the square tower, its attached dwelling, and the pier foundation, under a $4,740 contract.

James Clark, the first keeper, was described by a local newspaper as "the right man in the right place," though few "would care to exchange places with him, in his lonely and cheerless situation." Keeper Clark complained that the lighthouse shook in stormy weather and asked that the structure be more firmly secured to the block so it would not topple in winter gales.

Harry G. Maloney was serving as keeper of the lighthouse in 1895 when he reported several sightings of a sea serpent. Keeper Maloney claimed, "I saw something swimming through the Bay the like of which I never saw before and have not seen since. It was not a seal, because a seal will go under once in a while, but this fish or animal, or whatever it was, never put his head under water. It was around here for about a week…" Maloney once set after the creature in the station's boat, hoping to get a shot at it, but he said he "might as well have chased a comet."

In 1919, a gas installation, controlled by a sun valve, was placed in the lighthouse, and its keeper was withdrawn. A red skeletal tower replaced the lighthouse in 1957.

Tongue Shoal Lighthouse at high tide. (Library and Archives Canada)

21. Chamcook

Chamcook Lighthouse after being destroyed by lightning on December 2, 1945. (Canadian Coast Guard)

Chamcook Lighthouse was built in 1914 under the direction of C. N. Breen and D. J. Gallagher for $1,341.04. The square, wooden tower, with a height of 8.3 metres, used a fourth-order lens to produce a flashing light.

The station was automated in 1921. On December 2, 1945, the tower was struck by lightning and destroyed.

22. Midjik Bluff

Midjik Bluff Lighthouse, 1934. (Canadian Coast Guard)

The lighthouse atop Midjik Bluff, situated near the entrance to St. George's Harbour, first beamed forth its fixed white light on April 1, 1876. The square, pyramidal lighthouse, painted white with a brown lantern, stood 8.8 metres tall, but the bluff gave it a lofty focal plane of 39.6 metres.

John McDiarmid received $50 for the necessary land; C. Messenett was paid $674 for erecting the tower; the lighting apparatus was billed at $526.42; and after various incidentals were included, the total cost of the lighthouse came to $1,330.42.

The lighthouse was automated in 1921. The wooden tower was damaged by a lightning strike in 1956 and replaced by a red skeletal tower in 1957. The light was discontinued in 1970.

23. Green's Point (L'etete Passage)

L'etete Passage fog alarm, 1901. (Library and Archives Canada)

Bounded by Green's Point on the east and Macs Island on the west, L'etete Passage was a thoroughfare used by vessels to enter Passamaquoddy Bay en route to the wharves at St. Andrews, St. Stephen, and St. George. L'etete is derived from the French "la tête," which means "the head," and likely refers to the headlands that bracket the passage.

In 1878, Parliament appropriated $1,500 for a steam-powered fog alarm at L'etete Passage, and D. W. Clark constructed the fog alarm building and a reservoir to supply the needed water. A fog trumpet was procured from the Neptune Fog Horn Company of Quebec and placed in operation in 1879. Every thirty seconds during thick weather, fogs, and snowstorms, the trumpet would sound seven-second blasts.

Angus Fisher built a substantial two-storey dwelling in 1879 for the fog alarm engineer, a position Samuel Craig held for just a few months before being transferred to Head Harbour in late 1879. Neil Seely then served at Green's Point until 1882 when he was replaced by George Helms.

The Green's Point Lightstation is open to the public during summer months and offers a popular guest house rental.

As a retired sea captain, George Helms understood the risk presented by navigational hazards in the area and was familiar with many sailors of the North Atlantic. One of these sailors was Charles Dines, who faced a personal dilemma when his wife died in 1869, leaving behind a three-year-old son, Sidney S. Dines. Unable to take Sidney along on his sailings, Charles decided to allow his friends George and Elizabeth Helms to adopt him. Sidney was made an assistant engineer at L'etete Passage in 1884, earning an annual salary of $150.

Besides the dwelling and fog alarm building, a coal shed was provided to store the roughly ninety tons of soft coal needed to run the boiler each year. In 1903, C. L. McKeen built the present wooden octagonal lighthouse at a contract price of eight hundred dollars. The tower was constructed at St. Andrews in eight sections, which were then transported to the point by scow and assembled northwest of the fog alarm building. Topped by a red, octagonal, iron lantern, the tower measures 13.1 metres tall and originally exhibited a fixed white light from a seventh-order lens.

During the winter of 1907, Captain Helms passed away, and Sidney Dines was appointed head keeper. While George Helms served nearly twenty-five years as keeper, his adopted son logged fifty-three years of service at Green's Point, twenty-nine of those as head keeper. Sidney married Mary Gates in 1887, and they were blessed with five daughters and four boys, along with two adopted children. On November 7, 1936, Sidney S. Dines received a medal for his long and faithful service from His Majesty King George VI.

In the fall of 1920, a new fog alarm building was constructed, and a Class "B" diaphone, powered by oil engines, was installed the following year. Keeper Dines had little faith in the newfangled gas motors and might have retired if his son Prescott hadn't pitched in to keep them operating. Prescott Dines replaced his father as keeper in 1936.

Though electricity arrived at nearby L'etete in 1937, Prescott recalls it didn't reach the station until 1952 because a neighbour wanted to charge the power company ten dollars per pole to cross his land.

Gale force winds occasionally buffeted exposed Green's Point. In October of 1869, the Saxby Gale struck New Brunswick, and a high tide coupled with hurricane-force winds cut off the point from the mainland. Prescott remembers one winter gale that blew his mother right out of a one-horse sleigh, but thanks to her large buffalo robe, she suffered no harm. "One of my mother's guests chose a very windy day to visit us at the Lighthouse and consequently, the Privy house," Prescott recalls. "No sooner had the gentle lady finished her business and exited from the Privy—when an extra

Travel Instructions: From Highway 1, just west of St. George, take NB 172 south for 16 kilometres toward the Deer Island ferry. Just before the ferry, a road on your left leads a short distance to Green's Point Lighthouse. A museum in the keeper's dwelling is open between mid-June and Labour Day from 9 A.M. to 5 P.M. The vacation cottage on the grounds can be rented by calling 506-755-3630.

Established: 1879 (present tower 1903)

Position: 45.03887 N, -66.89157 W

Light: Inactive since 1999

Tower Height: 13.1 metres

Focal Plane: 14.6 metres

Description: White octagonal tower, red lantern

big puff of wind blew the little building over the bank and onto the rocks below."

In 1962, a year before his retirement, Prescott, who weighed about 130 pounds, experienced the full force of the wind first-hand: "The wind was of gale proportions and it took complete and absolute charge of me. The next thing I knew I found myself down on all fours among the rocks, alone and much bruised. I made up my mind, then and there, that as soon as possible I would retire, while I still had two feet and legs on which to go."

In 1963, the original dwelling was demolished to make way for modern keeper's quarters. Two new houses were finished the following year, one on the spot of the old dwelling and the other on the eastern side of the point. The eastern dwelling was sold and relocated to Back Bay in 1979.

In the late 1980s, Green's Point became a monitoring station for several other lighthouses in the area. While most of the nearby stations were de-staffed, four full-time keepers were needed at Green's Point to cover all the lights.

After news of the planned de-staffing of Green's Point leaked out in 1995, concerned citizens formed the Green's Point Light Association to maintain the station as an educational and recreational facility. An informational meeting was held in the remaining keeper's dwelling on November 10, 1996, and with growing support, an agreement allowing use of the property was signed between the association and the Canadian Coast Guard on December 4, 1996. The following July, a marine and coastal interpretive centre, which has displays on the lighthouse, coastal flora and fauna, and local marine industries, was opened in the keeper's dwelling.

After being fully automated since 1996, Green's Point Light was officially decommissioned on September 8, 1999, though a fog alarm remains in use. Ownership of the lighthouse and station was transferred to Green's Point Light Association in July 2008. A Coast Guard monitoring station on the property has served as a vacation rental since 2002 to raise money for maintaining the property.

24. Bliss Island

Samuel Bliss was making his living as a merchant in Greenfield, Massachusetts, when the Proscription Act of 1778 banished him from the colony for being loyal to the crown. After fighting with the British Army during the Revolutionary War, Samuel was rewarded in 1784 with five hundred acres fronting the river in L'Etang, New Brunswick, and later with a nearby island that is still known as Bliss Island.

Samuel built a fine home on his island before passing away in 1803 in his early fifties. Starting in the 1990s, Professor David Black of the University of New Brunswick led excavations of the Samuel Bliss homestead and discovered that he must have had an extensive farming operation as bones from pigs, chickens, cattle, and sheep were uncovered.

Head Harbour Lighthouse was established in 1828 to mark the southern side of the northern entrance to Passamaquoddy Bay, and it was only logical that another lighthouse would eventually be built to mark the entrance's northern side. Located eight kilometres northeast of Head Harbour Lighthouse, with only open water in between, Bliss Island was a natural site for this second lighthouse, which could also mark the protected anchorages at Bliss Harbour and L'Etang Harbour.

Bliss Island Lighthouse, 1934. (Canadian Coast Guard)

The Bliss Island Lighthouse, 2002.

Travel Instructions: As the island is well offshore, the lighthouse is best seen by boat. Captain Riddle's (506-752-2009) offers lighthouse cruises that pass by Bliss Island.

Established: 1871 (present tower 1964)

Position: 45.01809 N, -66.85061 W

Light: Red flash every 4 s

Tower Height: 11.6 metres

Focal Plane: 15.4 metres

Description: White rectangular tower rising from corner of one-storey white building, red lantern

Bliss Island Lighthouse was constructed in 1871 and commenced operation on December 1 of that year, with Jarvis Clarke as keeper. The lighthouse was a square wooden tower, painted white, and exhibited a fixed red light produced by five flat-wick lamps backed by reflectors. In 1872, a signal gun, which was owned by the International Steamboat Company and had been in use at Point Lepreau, was transferred to Bliss Island for firing during foggy weather.

In 1874, the marine department paid $250 for the land on which the lighthouse stood and an adjacent lot. Much of this six-acre parcel was wooded and could provide a source of fuel for the keeper, and when cleared, could accommodate additional buildings. As it was, the keeper and his family lived in the cramped lighthouse, where "the smell from the oil and lamps was anything but agreeable or pleasant."

Keeper Clarke made numerous appeals for a detached dwelling or at least an addition to the present quarters to house his large family. This request was fulfilled when James Donohue was paid $745 in 1876 to construct a dwelling near the lighthouse.

Keeper Clarke's next request was in 1878 for a supply of medicine and directions for use as members of his family were "not very healthy." Two years later, Keeper Clarke passed away and was replaced by Hugh Maloney.

On January 15, 1901, the characteristic of Bliss Island Light was changed from fixed red to fixed white, which greatly increased its range and usefulness. In 1903, an octagonal iron lantern replaced the lighthouse's original wooden lantern, and the height of the tower was increased to 12.2 metres.

Two dwellings and a combination lighthouse and fog alarm building were completed in August 1965, and the next month, lighthouse authorities received the following letter from Marblehead, Massachusetts:

On our way back from the St. John River where we spent three weeks cruising on our ketch in August, we were fog-bound in Bliss Island for five days. The lighthouse keeper, Mr. Roy Hatt, and his wife were most hospitable, even supplying us with eggs and sugar. They also invited us over to see the new lighthouse and big new foghorn. I would like you to know how much we appreciate their kindness to us.

Sincerely, Mr. & Mrs. Peter Vosburgh, ketch 'Albacore'

Keeper Hatt was commended for his actions and praised for being a fine representative of the department.

During the night of August 18, 1966, the Hatts were away from the island when a kerosene refrigerator caused a fire in the primary dwelling. Quick action by the assistant keeper and his wife prevented a total loss of the building, but initial estimates were $3,200 in damage plus a "fairly high claim from the lightkeeper

Bliss Island Lighthouse, as seen from a whale-watching boat at half tide.

for furniture, clothing, linen, etc which had either been burned or ruined by smoke or water." Keeper Hatt submitted a detailed claim for $2,231.75, which included "1 box greeting cards, 1 box hasty notes, and 2 boxes serviettes," however he received just $710.85 along with an admonition to obtain his own insurance.

H. L. Cook was appointed principal keeper in 1968 and served in that capacity until he suffered a massive heart attack on April 30, 1982, and was forced to take an early retirement. Assistant keeper E. A. Matheson took charge of the station until it was de-staffed on June 30, 1987.

FUNDY COAST

25. Pea Point

The department of marine entered into a contract in 1876 for a lighthouse on Pea Island, off the southern tip of Blacks Harbour Peninsula. The work was nearly complete when John H. Harding, the marine agent at Saint John, visited the site in September 1877 and issued the following report: "It is situated at the eastern entrance to L'Etang Harbour. During my stay at this place I had an opportunity of examining more fully this safe and spacious port. Without exception it is one of the very finest harbours in the Bay of Fundy...The two lights, one at the western (Bliss Island Lighthouse), and the other at the eastern entrance to this extensive and sheltered harbour, are two lights of the greatest value to the marine service of the Bay of Fundy."

The original Pea Point Lighthouse consisted of a wooden, square, pyramidal tower, 9.4 metres high, with an attached one-and-a-half-storey dwelling. The total cost of the lighthouse came to $1,905.17, and Keeper Alexander Davidson first exhibited the light on January 1, 1878.

When Harding visited the lighthouse in 1878, he reported, "The workmanship throughout is of the roughest kind, and ought not, in my opinion, to have passed the local inspector, though I have not the specification before me to refer to. I can scarcely believe that it has been finished according to specification and contract." Harding also found the green light, which had been selected to distinguish Pea Point from other lights in the area, to be inadequate. Further proof of the light's deficiency was the following complaint by J. N. Purdy, captain of the steamship *Newfield*: "The light at present exhibited at Pea Point is not at all suitable, as a green light does not show for any great distance, and is liable to be mistaken for a vessel's starboard light."

The issue with the green light must have been resolved, as Pea Point would retain its green signature for several more years. In 1914, a fourth-order dioptric lens was installed in the lighthouse, and the light's signature was changed to fixed white.

Pea Point Lighthouse atop foundation of earlier lighthouse.

Original Pea Point Lighthouse with addition. (Michel Forand)

Travel Instructions: From Route 1, take Exit 60 and travel south on Route 176 for 10 kilometres through Blacks Harbour toward the Grand Manan ferry terminal. Just before the terminal, a gated dirt road leads off to the left. Park and follow this dirt road on foot for 0.6 kilometres from where, at low tide, you can access Pea Island. Aim for an old foundation, which will put you on a footpath that leads to the lighthouse. The lighthouse is also visible from the Grand Manan Ferry.

Established: 1878 (present structure 1965)

Position: 45.03916 N, -66.80846 W

Light: Fixed white

Tower Height: 10.6 metres

Focal Plane: 17.2 metres

Description: White rectangular tower rising from corner of one-storey white building, red lantern

Pea Island was purchased for $75 from a Mr. Bennett, who was also willing to sell five acres on the tip of the nearby peninsula for $150. The purchase of this property was recommended so "the keeper might have an opportunity to raise some farm produce to assist in supplying himself and family." It was believed that the purchase price would be quickly offset as the products of the land "would fully supplement a low salary, while without a small piece of land to work, the Department may find it difficult to retain a keeper without an increase of salary."

Various repairs and upgrades were made at Pea Point through the years. The lighthouse received an addition in 1885, and in 1895 the oil house was repaired. In 1898, the reflectors were resilvered, the glass in the lantern was reglazed, and a new cement floor was laid in the basement of the tower.

Keeper Elias C. Dickson was provided a hand fog-horn in 1900 to answer the fog signals of vessels in the vicinity. In 1929, a rectangular building was built east of the lighthouse to house a more powerful fog signal. Two oil engines powered a diaphone that would sound two blasts of 3.5 seconds duration every minute when needed. According to a November 1929 article in the *Saint Croix Courier*, the fog alarm was expected to "be a great help for the Connors Brothers sardine boats making the harbour entrance."

After serving in the First World War, Andrew Murray returned home, married Myrtle Brown a few months later, and on November 1, 1920, became keeper at Pea Point Lighthouse. The Murrays raised a family of twelve children on the island, nine of whom were born in the lighthouse between 1923 and 1939. Keeper Murray left Pea Island for most of 1942 to serve in the Second World War, but resumed his position on April 1, 1943, and served until his retirement in 1946.

A two-storey dwelling was constructed on the island in 1950, and then in 1964 a contract for $20,850 was entered into with Cardinal Construction to demolish all existing buildings and to construct a new dwelling and combination light tower and fog alarm building. Work was completed by August of 1965. The station was de-staffed in 1989 and the bungalow was sold and relocated to West Saint John.

26. Lighthouse Point
(Beaver Harbour, Drews Head)

Original Beaver Harbour Lighthouse. (Library and Archives Canada)

This fibreglass tower replaced the 1967 skeletal tower in 1984.

Beaver Harbour was settled in 1783 by a group of Loyalists who fled the United States at the close of the Revolutionary War. By June 4, 1785, when the town was incorporated, it had eight hundred residents. A great fire in 1790 destroyed all but one home in the town, causing many of the original settlers to relocate elsewhere, but Beaver Harbour was slowly rebuilt.

Parliament appropriated funds for a lighthouse at Beaver Harbour in 1874, and a site on Drews Head was selected that fall and purchased from Lewis Holmes for $100. Messrs. W. B. Deacon and John Ward of Shediac built the lighthouse, which consisted of a square, wooden tower, attached to a dwelling, under a $1,650 contract.

Ezra Munro was appointed the first keeper of the lighthouse at an annual salary of $250, and he made the inaugural lighting on January 15, 1876. The lighthouse tower stood eleven metres tall, and its fixed white light guided vessels into Beaver Harbour, which was frequently used as a harbour of refuge.

John H. Harding, the marine agent at Saint John, visited Drews Head in 1876 and reported that he was both surprised and pleased to see the improvements made since the lighthouse was built. Keeper Munro, aided by his family, had cleared the property and built a small wharf for landing supplies. Munro was credited

for being "very attentive to his work, and desirous of discharging his duties to the best of his ability." In 1877, Keeper Munro requested a one-hundred-dollar raise, as even with the most rigid economy he was unable to support his large family.

In 1882, Ezra Munro exchanged assignments with Edward Snell of Southwest Wolf Island Lighthouse. In doing so, Munro's salary was increased to five hundred

Travel Instructions: From Route 1, take Exit 60 and follow Route 778 south for 6.2 kilometres. After passing through Beaver Harbour, turn left onto Lighthouse Road, drive 0.5 kilometres, and park in the turnout area. Pass through the gate and continue 0.3 kilometres to the lighthouse.

Established: 1876 (present structure 1984)

Position: 45.06297 N, -66.73306 W

Light: White, on 7 s, eclipse 8 s

Tower Height: 8.6 metres

Focal Plane: 14.2 metres

Description: White cylindrical tower, red lantern

dollars, which helped support his family. Keeper Snell served at Drews Head for nearly ten years until his unexpected passing in February of 1892. In his obituary, Snell was remembered as "a splendid specimen of physical manhood—a typical 'old sea dog.'"

In 1905, a lamp and seventh-order lens replaced the antiquated lamps and reflectors used in the lantern room. The new lamp burned petroleum vapour under an incandescent mantle to produce a fixed white light.

Despite a significant movement within the community to save the original combination dwelling and tower, a skeletal tower replaced it in 1967. The present fibreglass tower dates from 1984.

Until recent years, this lighthouse was known as Drews Head; now, it has the appropriate but non-distinct designation of Lighthouse Point.

27. Point Lepreau

Situated roughly midway between Saint John and St. Andrews, Point Lepreau juts into the Bay of Fundy, presenting a significant obstacle for coastal shipping.

The commissioners of lighthouses proposed a lighthouse at Point Lepreau as early as 1827; however, it wasn't until 1831 that they were granted £500 to cover construction.

Point Lepreau Lighthouse was unique in that it exhibited two lights. The light atop the tower was composed of five lamps in twenty-three-inch reflectors, while five lamps with fifteen-inch reflectors produced a second light, displayed from a lower floor of the tower. In 1840, the lower light was moved to the ground floor, so the two lights were less likely to merge into one when observed at a great distance.

The station's first keeper, Daniel Pettingell, was provided guns and powder in 1848 to answer the signals of vessels. After leaving Saint John in foggy weather, steamers would run a prescribed period of time. Then, when they believed they were off Point Lepreau, they would ring their bell or sound their whistle. Upon being answered by the gun at Point Lepreau, these vessels could continue on with confidence, having obtained a new departure. The fog alarm at Point Lepreau was greatly improved in 1869, when a steam fog signal was established. The total cost for the fog whistle and building, along with a dwelling for the engineer and a well for

Point Lepreau Lighthouse that served from 1899 to 1956. (Michel Forand)

water, was $3,702. J. Christy was hired as the first engineer for the fog alarm at an annual salary of $400, while George Thomas Sr. was serving as lighthouse keeper.

New lamps with mammoth flat-wick burners and new reflectors were installed in the two lantern rooms in 1873, and the resulting light could be seen at Head Harbour Lighthouse, a distance of thirty-eight kilometres. This improved light came at a cost, as the new lamps consumed four quarts, one pint, and one gill of oil nightly—nearly double that of the old lamps.

A telegraph station was established in the keeper's dwelling in 1874, and the daughter of Keeper Thomas was hired as the operator. Miss Thomas would dispatch a weather report to Saint John twice a day along with

The 1958 concrete Point Lepreau Lighthouse.

Travel Instructions: The nearby nuclear power plant restricts access to the lighthouse by land and air, but it can be viewed by boat.

Established: 1831 (present structure 1958)

Position: 45.05881 N, -66.45869 W

Light: White, on 1 s, eclipse 4 s

Tower Height: 17.6 metres

Focal Plane: 25.5 metres

Description: Octagonal tower with red and white horizontal bands, red lantern

a record of all vessels passing the point. A five-room addition was made to the dwelling the following year to compensate for the space allocated to the telegraph office. As Keeper Thomas had a large family, the extra space was greatly appreciated.

After visiting Point Lepreau in 1878, John H. Harding, marine agent at Saint John, had the following praise for Keeper Thomas:

> *The reflectors of both lights have a bright and high polish, and reflect, like mirrors, objects put in front of them; we have none like them on this coast. I could not but ask Mr. Thomas how he obtained such a brilliant polish, and he replied that he occasionally used the silver wash supplied by me some few years ago. He was at first disposed to throw it away, believing that it did no good, but Mr. Thomas being a thoroughly intelligent and practical man, was determined to give it a fair trial before condemning it. He therefore persevered, using it as directed, and it was not long before he found the reflectors getting brighter and more brilliant, and by perseveringly continuing its use, they were in time covered with a new coating of silver, fully as bright, if not more so, than when they first came out of the silversmith's battery.*

The other keepers who received the wash had given up on the process before the desired effect was achieved.

Keeper Thomas passed away in 1884, and his son was appointed keeper in his stead. The following year a new fog alarm building was erected on the tip of the point in front of the lighthouse at a cost of $1,987 to house an improved Champion foghorn. Obscured by the new fog alarm building, the lower light was discontinued in November 1886.

In January 1898, a fire at Point Lepreau claimed the lighthouse, fog alarm, and thirty tons of coal. A new fog alarm building was constructed on the foundation of its predecessor, and the new signal commenced operation on March 9, 1898. A Chance anchor lens was displayed from a mast as a temporary light until a new octagonal, wooden lighthouse was activated on October 1, 1899. This tower measured 16.5 metres from its sills to the vane on the lantern, was painted in red and white horizontal bands, and displayed a revolving white light. Francis Cassidy constructed the tower at a cost of $1,325, but the quality of his work was so poor that parts of it had to be redone to pass inspection.

The foghorn was replaced by a diaphone in 1905, necessitating the enlargement of the fog alarm building. An electric lighting plant was installed in 1913, and a new dwelling was erected at the station in 1921.

During a storm in December of 1956, Point Lepreau Lighthouse was struck by lightning and destroyed. The present concrete tower, which retains the octagonal shape and the red and white horizontal bands of its predecessors, was built on the point in 1958. The lighthouse was de-staffed in 1980, and since that time all other station buildings have been removed.

After Point Lepreau Generating Station commenced operation in 1983, access to the lighthouse has been difficult, especially after 9/11.

28. Dipper Harbour

A square, white tower with a red roof was built on the southern point of Campbell Island in 1888 to guide vessels into Dipper Harbour. The lighthouse exhibited a fixed white light at an elevation of 9.1 metres and was first lit on July 1, 1888.

The light was changed to red in 1889, and in 1891 an additional window was added to the lantern to help mariners make the inner harbour. The tower was destroyed on September 11, 1954.

This small tower served Dipper Harbour from 1888 to 1954. (Library and Archives Canada)

29. Chance Harbour

In 1915, day labourers working under D. H. Mawhinney completed a square, wooden tower on Reef Point to mark the western side of the entrance to Chance Harbour. A cylindrical tower with red and white horizontal bands and an exposed light replaced the original lighthouse around 1969 and was still active in 2011.

Chance Harbour Lighthouse, 1935. (Canadian Coast Guard)

30. Musquash Head

Original Musquash Head Lighthouse.
(Library and Archives Canada)

Musquash Head Lighthouse in 2011.

Musquash is an archaic name for a muskrat, derived from the Abenaki word *mòoskwas*. Musquash Harbour is located just a few kilometres west of Saint John, and in 2007, the Musquash Estuary, which extends from the mouth of the harbour to the head of tides on the east and west branches of the Musquash River, was declared New Brunswick's first marine protected area. Now, the muskrats and other wildlife that frequent the estuary will benefit from twenty-seven square kilometres of protected habitat.

The cliffs of Musquash Head define the eastern side of the entrance to Musquash Harbour, and in 1878 Parliament appropriated $2,000 for a lighthouse on the headland to mark the harbour. The total cost of Musquash Head Lighthouse, a keeper's dwelling attached to a square, wooden tower, came to $3,271. Keeper Charles P. Hamm first displayed the catoptric light, which showed green to seaward and white into the harbour, on February 15, 1879.

The village of Musquash, described in 1875 as having a sawmill, three stores, a hotel, and a population of two hundred, was the centre of commerce on Musquash Harbour. Six years later, the village had five sawmills and had just received the service of the Grand Southern Railway.

At some point after 1904 the light's characteristic and the tower's daymark were altered. The 1916 *List of*

Lights indicates that the lighthouse could be identified by a group of four flashes every thirty seconds and by red and white horizontal bands on the tower; the tower was originally painted all white.

The present octagonal concrete tower was built in 1959, and a foghorn was added to the station in 1967 after the one at Tiner Point, five kilometres to the east, was discontinued. By November of 1979, one

Travel Instructions: From Route 1 west of Saint John, take Exit 112 and follow King William Road 8 kilometres south to its terminus at Colson Cove Generating Station. Bear right onto a dirt road and continue 2.3 kilometres to a red gate on your left. Park here and follow the dirt road for 1.2 kilometres to reach the lighthouse.

Established: 1879 (present tower 1959)

Position: 45.14364 N, -66.23728 W

Light: White, on 1 s, eclipse 2 s

Tower Height: 13.9 metres

Focal Plane: 35.1 metres

Description: White octagonal tower with red horizontal band, red lantern

of the keeper's dwellings had been sold and moved to Hampton. The lighthouse was automated in the early 1980s, and the last keeper left in 1987. Soon after, the last dwelling was removed from the site.

July 21, 2008, was an auspicious day for the New Brunswick lighthouse community. Guests gathered inside the New Brunswick Museum to witness the divestiture of Musquash Head Lighthouse and Green's Point Lighthouse from the department of fisheries and oceans (DFO) to local groups. Though unable to attend, Patrick Donovan, project coordinator for Musquash Head Lightstation, prepared the following statement:

We have not yet determined what our exact plans for the property are, but we are committed to protecting the natural beauty of the site. To that end, we will retain control of approximately 12 acres of land directly around the lighthouse and we have agreed to place the remaining 98 acres into the trust of the Nature Conservancy of Canada (NCC). There are many examples where magnificent lighthouse properties have been opened to the public with little forethought and the result is often huge parking lots congested with cars and recreational vehicles, gift shops and all manner of tourist trappings. Partnering with NCC is the first step in ensuring that Musquash Head never falls prey to that type of development. We intend to take a slow, methodical and environmentally responsible approach to any future development. We will consult with other groups and we will take the time to get it right. It may take awhile but the end result will be something that the people of the Fundy Region will be able to take great pride in.

31. Negro Point

In 1878, an open-frame hexagonal tower, painted white and surmounted by a red lantern, was established near the outer end of the recently completed breakwater that extended 686 metres from Negro Point in Saint John toward Partridge Island. Keeper Elijah Ross first exhibited the tower's fixed red light on July 24 of that year.

After a gale in January 1879 severely damaged the breakwater, the tower was removed, and a temporary pole light was exhibited for a few years. With the breakwater repaired, the original tower was placed atop a circular stone pier near the breakwater's outer limit, and its fixed red dioptric light was activated on November 24, 1883. The light was changed to fixed white in 1896 and automated in 1918. The tower was demolished around 1922.

Calls to extend the breakwater to reach Partridge Island were made in the 1920s, but the work was not accomplished until the 1960s.

Negro Point Breakwater Lighthouse circa 1895. (New Brunswick Museum, 1967.25D)

32. Partridge Island

A committee was appointed by the New Brunswick House of Assembly in 1787 to determine a proper place for a lighthouse at Saint John and to estimate the cost of its construction. The following year, the committee reported that it had selected Partridge Island, situated at the entrance to the inner harbour, and believed the lighthouse could be erected for £120.

A bill passed by the House in 1788 required that vessels greater than fifteen tons belonging to the port of Saint John should pay a lighthouse duty at the rate of two pence per ton, while foreign vessels would pay twice that rate. The duty was not to take effect until after the lighthouse commenced operation, which it did in 1791 with Samuel Duffy serving as its first keeper.

In 1812, £200 was granted to repair and enlarge the keeper's dwelling, dig a well, construct an oil vat, and build a wharf at the island. Another £200 was allocated in 1831 to have a fog bell erected on Partridge Island.

In January of 1832, a fire that originated in the lantern room floor, through which a stovepipe passed, destroyed Partridge Island Lighthouse. A lantern was hung on the western yardarm of a signal-post, part of a signal station that broadcasted the arrival of ships at Saint John, until a new lighthouse could be completed.

According to records from 1833, £316 was spent in constructing and furnishing a new octagonal lighthouse. In 1840, the sides of this tower were alternately painted red and white, giving the tower its characteristic daymark that persists to this day. The new tower measured 12.2 metres tall and had a focal plane of 36.3 metres. A fog bell was initially attached to the lighthouse, but as this prevented it from being heard at a sufficient distance, £40 was allocated in 1835 for a fog bell tower.

A new keeper's house was built in 1841. The previous dwelling was at some distance from the lighthouse, which made accessing the tower in inclement weather a great difficulty for the keeper.

Second Partridge Island Lighthouse, 1856.
(New Brunswick Museum, 1967.25A)

Firings at the nearby battery impacted the lighthouse and those living at the station. In 1861, plate glass in the lantern room had to be replaced after a salute was fired in honour of the arrival of His Royal Highness the Prince of Wales.

When a lighthouse was proposed for Cape Enrage, a new lantern was ordered from England for Partridge Island Lighthouse, and its old lantern was installed at Cape Enrage. This larger lantern allowed the installation of an extra bank of reflectors above the existing bank in 1841, bringing the total number of lamps and twenty-three-inch reflectors to fifteen.

In 1853, Robert Foulis proposed that his invention for producing gas from coal be used to fuel the light on Partridge Island. For the sum of £75, Foulis agreed to superintend the manufacture and installation of his gas-producing apparatus with materials provided by the commissioners. Then, for a period of four years, Foulis would keep the apparatus in working order and instruct

The 1880 tower as it appeared in 1942 among the many buildings present during the Second World War. (Canadian Coast Guard)

the keeper in the manufacture of gas for an annual salary of £50.

After £542 had been spent for its manufacture and installation, the gas lighting apparatus commenced operation in August of 1853, but then in January, the water used to produce the gas froze, and oil had to be used once again in the lamps. The interior of the gas house was soon plastered, rendering it frost-proof, and the manufacturing of gas resumed.

During 1855 and 1856, the annual cost of using gas was roughly £100 more than using oil. Although the light was certainly more brilliant, the gas-making experiment was eventually abandoned.

Recognizing that a fog alarm in poor visibility was more important than a light in clear conditions, the commissioners responsible for navigational aids were always open to improvements in this area. Over the years, a cannon, a fog bell (struck by various methods), and a metal gong were tried.

In April of 1859, T. T. Vernon Smith submitted to Isaac Woodward, superintendent of lighthouses for the Bay of Fundy, a drawing of a steam whistle, similar to that used on locomotives, to guide vessels during foggy weather. Smith estimated that this device, consisting of a whistle, a boiler, and a speaking tube to focus the sound, could be manufactured for around £250. Fleming and Humbert agreed to make a device according to Smith's plan and install it on Partridge Island for £300. In addition, the two men guaranteed that the whistle would be heard for nine kilometres or they would forfeit their pay.

With the blessing of the chamber of commerce of Saint John, Fleming and Humbert were authorized to build the steam whistle. During a test of the whistle on November 14, 1859, ships that were situated nine and sixteen kilometres from the island were able to hear the signal.

The test was performed without a structure to house the steam whistle or a method for supplying water, but these necessary additions were completed before the following spring, when the steam whistle commenced operation. Captains of passenger steamers, pilots of Saint John, masters of steam tugs, and the Saint John harbour master all signed a certificate stating that the whistle was "superior to any thing heretofore adopted as a warning to vessels approaching the land during fog." The chamber of commerce passed a resolution congratulating Smith on his efficient and useful invention of the world's first steam foghorn.

There was just one problem. The invention did not belong to Vernon Smith. Smith had adopted Robert Foulis's plan, reportedly at the prompting of Isaac Woodward. Foulis was responsible for the gas works on the island and had been telling the commissioners of lights since 1854 that a steam whistle would be the best way to signal vessels during foggy conditions.

Shortly after the steam fog whistle went into operation, Robert Foulis started petitioning the government to recognize him as its inventor, but it took years of letter writing before he received his due credit. A committee of the House of Assembly appointed in 1864 to investigate the matter, "after a careful perusal of the papers placed before" them, ultimately concluded "that Robert Foulis, Civil Engineer, Saint John, is the true inventor of the practical application of the Steam Horn or Whistle now in such successful and beneficial operation at Partridge Island, which, although three miles distant from the City is distinctly and loudly heard throughout its bounds."

Foulis had also proposed that unique sounds and intervals could be deployed to help differentiate fog signal stations, much as had been done with distinctive light characteristics for lighthouses. Foulis died in poverty in 1866. A plaque recognizing his achievement was placed on Partridge Island in 1925.

Partridge Island Lighthouse as viewed from the Saint John–Digby ferry. Saint John's Carleton Martello Tower is in the background.

It took some time to fine-tune the fog whistle installation, but this was finally achieved, and from 1862 to 1865, the fog whistle averaged 888 hours and 47 minutes of operation each year.

Besides being the site for New Brunswick's first lighthouse, Partridge Island was also home to North America's first quarantine station. A great influx of Irish immigrants occurred during the 1840s, when, due to the Irish Potato Famine, more than thirty thousand people were processed at the island. Over six hundred immigrants were buried on the island in 1847, when the hospital was so overwhelmed that the infirm were forced to lie on the bare ground. The island continued to serve as a quarantine station until 1941.

Alexander Reed, who had succeeded his father as keeper, petitioned the government in 1848 for compensation for "losses sustained in consequence of depredations committed upon his property on the Island, by the numerous Emigrants landed thereon during the past year by direction of the Public Authorities." In 1855, Keeper Reed petitioned for an increase in salary as his children were deprived of school, and the sick immigrants exposed his family to infectious diseases.

Due to poor health, Keeper Reed resigned as keeper in 1873, after nearly forty years of service. James Wilson, who had been the engineer for the fog alarm since 1860, was placed in charge of both the light and alarm.

In 1872, twelve new lamps, nine using mammoth flatwicks and three using the largest round-wicks available, were installed in the lantern replacing lamps that used a half-inch flat-wick. The change to these new lamps resulted in the consumption of an additional 118 gallons of oil each month, but the improved light gave much satisfaction.

The system of lamps and reflectors was replaced in 1887 with a dioptric lens, housed in a new lantern. In 1911, the height of the lighthouse was increased by 2.7 metres through the addition of a concrete foundation under the tower. A third-order lens and a three-metre Canadian lantern were placed atop the tower in 1915.

A diaphone fog alarm was installed on Partridge Island in 1906 in a brick engine house, measuring twenty-seven by thirty-two feet, which had been completed the previous year. A water system used by the quarantine station was extended to the fog alarm in 1906, eliminating the need for wells, water tanks, and reservoirs.

The installation of an electric lighting plant was completed in 1914, and commercial electricity reached the station in 1926, when a submarine cable was laid to the island.

A completely new fog alarm installation had to be built on Partridge Island in 1953 to replace a building and equipment lost to fire.

The present lighthouse was constructed after its predecessor, a wooden octagonal tower reportedly built in 1880, was torn down in 1959. Ralph Eldridge started serving on Partridge Island as a second assistant in 1971. In 1977, he was appointed principal keeper and remained in this capacity until 1986, the year Partridge Island Lighthouse was de-staffed. The island's foghorn, so important to the history of the area, was silenced in 1999 despite huge public outcry.

Partridge Island, rich in both cultural and lighthouse history, is now designated as both a national and provincial historic site. A large Celtic cross was dedicated on the island in 1927 as a memorial to the two thousand Irish immigrants who perished there in "Black '47" along with James Patrick Collins, the young local doctor who cared for them and paid with his own life.

33. Saint John Harbour Beacon

To facilitate navigation into the port of Saint John, the Beacon Light was established atop a substantial wooden pier in the harbour in 1828. George Lane was an early keeper of the lighthouse, New Brunswick's second, and in 1833, he was receiving an annual salary of £100.

On the morning of January 7, 1867, the keeper of the Beacon Light was absent from the station when his two sons opened the coal cellar and discovered a fire. With much effort, the pair saved the four reflectors in the lantern room before fleeing the structure and watching helplessly as it burned down to water level. John McLachlan rebuilt the lighthouse and pier in 1868 for $2,300, which did not include the cost of a fourth-order French lens.

James E. Earle was appointed keeper in June of 1869. Just a few months later, during the night of October 4, a great "tidal wave," produced by what is now known as the Saxby Gale, swept over the lighthouse, tearing away the shingles and boards of the lower storey. During the storm, Keeper Earle sought refuge in the lantern, and when he was taken off the station the next day, he could not be convinced to resume his duties. The great wave swept away the station's boat, railing, and steps, and tore away planking on the pier, allowing large quantities of the pier's ballast to be washed away. Though the tower was heavily damaged, its light was shown as usual the following night. Repairs costing $898 were immediately initiated at the station.

In 1871, a large fog bell was installed at the lighthouse, and the keeper was instructed to sound the bell

Established in 1828 as New Brunswick's second lighthouse, the Harbour Beacon served for eighty-five years. Seen here at high tide, the foundation of this lighthouse was completely visible at low tide. (Canadian Coast Guard)

by hand "in response to the whistle of steamers or call of vessels seeking their way into the harbor." A bell tower was built on the southwest side of the pier in 1875, and clockwork machinery was installed to continuously toll the bell in foggy weather. The machinery had to be wound every two hours, and for one stretch during 1877, the bell was in constant operation for nearly three weeks. In 1905, the fog bell was relocated to the northeast end of the pier.

By 1896, the use of electric lights in Saint John made it hard to distinguish the Beacon Light, so its characteristic was changed from fixed white to fixed red. At the same time, the nearby Negro Point Breakwater Light was changed from fixed red to fixed white.

The Beacon Light was discontinued in 1913, as the bar on which it stood was dredged as part of harbour improvements at Saint John. Sand Point Range Lights were constructed nearby in 1914 to guide mariners into the harbour. New Burrell Johnson Iron Company provided a skeletal tower for the rear light, and a wooden tower was erected for the front light.

34. Saint John Coast Guard Base

This faux lighthouse was built in 1985 to represent the graceful octagonal wooden lighthouses in the region. Today it is a popular photo attraction for the thousands of cruise ship passengers that visit Saint John each year.

Travel Instructions: Located on the south side of the slip at Market Square at the foot of King Street in uptown Saint John. Parking is available in the immediate vicinity.

Established: 1985

Position: 45.27202 N, -66.06500 W

Light: Inactive (decorative light displayed)

Tower Height: 10 metres

Description: White octagonal tower, red lantern

Employees of the Saint John Coast Guard base built this octagonal wooden tower in 1985 under the direction of Larry Wilson, who served as base commander at the time. It is equipped with the 1911 lantern from Grindstone Island and an operational fourth-order Fresnel lens from Brier Island, Nova Scotia, though the light is not an official aid to navigation.

35. Digby Pier

Tower on pier with Digby in the background. (Library and Archives Canada)

Saint John's Market Square, with Digby Pier Lighthouse in the foreground and Saint John Coast Guard Base Lighthouse in the background at left.

This lighthouse, which dates from 1903, was originally located on Digby Pier in Nova Scotia. It was decommissioned when the pier was deemed unsafe, and then moved to the Saint John Coast Guard base in 1970. The tower was relocated to the renovated Market Slip area in 1983 and given to the city of Saint John.

Digby Pier Lighthouse has been maintained sporadically since being in Saint John, but it was given a major facelift in July of 2010.

Travel Instructions: Located adjacent to Loyalist Plaza and Market Slip directly behind the flags of Canada's ten provinces and three territories at the foot of King Street in uptown Saint John. Parking is available in the immediate vicinity.

Established: 1903

Position: 45.27264 N, -66.06463 W

Light: Inactive

Tower Height: 8 metres

Description: White square pyramidal tower, red-roofed lantern

36. Reed's Point

The recently relit Three Sisters Lamp shown with the Celtic cross that commemorates over two thousand Irish immigrants who died on Partridge Island in 1847.

Travel Instructions: Located at the intersection of Prince William Street and St. James Street in Saint John's south end. From Market Square in the city's uptown area, travel south on Water Street, past the cruise ship terminal, until you see the light on your left.

Established: 1842 (present lamppost 1997)

Position: 45.26713 N, -66.06043 W

Light: Red light seaward, white light landward

Description: Trident-shaped lamppost

Although Reed's Point Light may not qualify as a formal lighthouse, it is far too interesting an aid to navigation not to include. The original light at this location, erected in 1842, was a single lamp on an iron post and was positioned to line up with the steeple of Trinity Anglican Church to guide ships into the harbour.

In a letter dated January 12, 1847, the commissioners of lighthouses in the Bay of Fundy informed the Lieutenant-Governor of a new method for lighting the beacon at Reed's Point:

> *An arrangement has been made with the Gas Company in this City, to place a large Lantern with three Burners, at Reed's Point, to serve as a leading Light up the Harbor, the Light House Fund to pay for the additional consumption of Gas over what an ordinary Street Lamp burns, for which this Light also answers, and for which the City Corporation pays; this will be completed in a few days.*

In 1848, the Saint John Gas Company commissioned Alexander Campbell to replace the single lamp with three lamps on a trident. The lanterns displayed red to sea and white toward shore. If all three lights were seen separately then the ship was within the channel; if only one or two showed, then the ship was off course.

The three lights were converted from gas to electricity in 1896. In the spring of 1897, the lamppost was raised fifteen feet so that its three lights could be more clearly distinguished from the other electric lights along the harbour front.

After being restored by H. S. Gregory & Sons and Saint John Iron Works, the "three lamps" were rededicated on October 3, 1967, to the Saint John Harbour Pilots, and a plaque was added to commemorate the seven lives lost when Pilot Boat No. 6 was cut in two on January 14, 1957, by the SS *Fort Avalon* while on station in thick fog.

After 140 years of withstanding the elements, the old lamppost was replaced with a replica in 1997. In late 2008, St. Patrick's Square was completely renovated, and it now serves as the southern terminus of the popular Harbour Passage walking path. Reed's Point Light, affectionately known as "The Three Sisters," has become a familiar icon for the city of Saint John, and in September 2011, it was once again lit.

37. Cape Spencer

The original Cape Spencer Lighthouse, 1907. (Library and Archives Canada)

In an 1870 report, John Harley, inspector of lights for New Brunswick, recommended that a lighthouse be placed on Cape Spencer, a prominent headland situated 14.5 kilometres southeast of Saint John. A contract was awarded to Messrs. Clark and Stackhouse in 1871, and the resulting structure, built on the "Pitch of the Cape" over sixty metres above the bay, was first lit on June 15, 1873. The original wooden lighthouse consisted of a square, pyramidal tower and an attached keeper's dwelling.

To distinguish it from the fixed white light on Partridge Island, Cape Spencer Light employed two banks of lamps that revolved every three minutes to produce the following signature: forty-five seconds of red light, dark for forty-five seconds, forty-five seconds of white light, dark for forty-five seconds. The white light could reportedly be seen at a distance of thirty-eight kilometres, but the red light was only visible for sixteen kilometres. After a year of operation, a small stove was placed in the lighthouse during the winter months to keep frost out of the machinery that revolved the light.

George C. Blacklock was appointed the first keeper at Cape Spencer and was subsequently described as one

The 1918 concrete tower as it appeared in 1961. (Doug and Edith Andrews)

who "bestows the greatest care and attention upon his duties." Due in part to Keeper Blacklock's attentiveness, Cape Spencer had the reputation of being the best light on the Bay of Fundy. A boat was purchased for Keeper Blacklock to enable him to transport goods to the station, but landing at the station was dangerous and difficult.

The ten-acre lighthouse site at Cape Spencer was purchased from John Carney, who also owned the surrounding one hundred acres. Realizing that the hardwood trees on the adjoining land would provide an excellent fuel source for Cape Spencer and nearby light stations, the department of marine paid Mr. Carney $360 for the additional one hundred acres in 1875. Patrick Gorman was paid $40 for a right-of-way through his land, and a two-kilometre road connecting the lighthouse to the public highway was completed in 1877.

Cape Spencer's modern lighthouse and fog alarm, 2011.

A hand foghorn was given to the keeper in 1898, but a decade later, the station's fog signal was upgraded when a wooden fog alarm building was built to house a three-inch diaphone plant. A wooden dwelling was built for the fog alarm engineer, along with a 152-metre roadway to link the lighthouse and fog alarm.

The characteristic of Cape Spencer's light was changed to two flashes every thirty-six seconds in 1909, and an electric lighting plant was installed at the station in 1913.

During 1915 and 1916, a new fog alarm building and oil shed were constructed in preparation for new fog alarm machinery supplied by the Dominion Lighthouse Depot in Prescott, Ontario.

In 1918, F. H. Carson of Saint John built a new concrete tower to replace the old wooden lighthouse. This octagonal tower was painted white with a single horizontal red band about its middle and displayed a group flashing white light. The fog signal building, which was painted white and had a red roof, was situated southwest of the tower near the end of the cape. The fog alarm building burned to the ground on November 29, 1927, and a new building was erected the following year to take its place.

On September 15, 1961, a construction worker was killed while pouring concrete for new keeper's dwellings at Cape Spencer. The present circular fibreglass tower, with its upper half painted red and lower half painted white, entered service in 1983, replacing a tapered, skeletal tower that had been erected in 1971, after demolition of the concrete lighthouse.

Although just the modern tower and a fog alarm building remain at Cape Spencer, remnants of numerous old foundations scattered around the area attest to the fact that this was once an important station. Three 1960s-era keeper's dwellings are located alongside the road just before you reach the lighthouse.

38. Quaco Head

The 1883 Quaco Head lighthouse with attached dwelling.
(Canadian Coast Guard)

Quaco Head Lighthouse shrouded in fog, June 2011.

Previously named Quaco, St. Martins was a busy ship-building centre in the 1800s, when over five hundred vessels were launched there.

The New Brunswick government set aside £400 in 1834 for "erecting a Buoy, or Beacon on the Quaco Ledges," near St. Martins, but the commissioners of lights for the Bay of Fundy gained approval the following year to use the funds to construct a manned lighthouse instead. Thrum Cap, a prominent ledge located off the headland west of St. Martins, was selected as the site, and work on the lighthouse was carried out in 1835. The first Quaco Lighthouse was an octagonal tower, painted in red and white horizontal stripes, with an attached dwelling, and could be reached by foot at low tide. Its lighting apparatus, employing six lamps backed by twenty-four-inch reflectors, revolved once every twenty seconds to produce fourteen seconds of light followed by six seconds of darkness. The weights that powered the revolving machinery had to be wound up every four hours. A bell struck by the machinery each revolution alerted the keeper that the light was functioning properly.

Captain Thomas Lamb, who was appointed the first keeper of Gannet Rock Lighthouse in 1831, was transferred to Quaco Lighthouse, where he had the honour of being its first keeper as well. Keeper Lamb originally received an annual salary of £100, but this was raised to £150 in 1841 due to the "great privations and dangers" presented by the offshore station and the inability to raise a garden or keep a cow there. In 1842, a severe storm carried away a portion of the rock on which the lighthouse stood along with two boats.

In 1846, a lumber breastwork was built on the crumbling rock to protect the foundation of the lighthouse. Two years later, the height of the lighthouse was increased to fourteen metres by enlarging the base of the tower and installing a larger lantern room. A new set of six lamps and reflectors, imported from England, were installed in the new lantern in 1849, and the revolving machinery was replaced in 1850.

Keeper Lamb retired in 1868, and his assistant, William Love, was appointed head keeper at an annual salary of $400.

The Saxby Gale of October 1869 caused extensive damage to Quaco Lighthouse. Repairs amounting to $298 were completed, but it was noted that the soft sandstone of Thrum Cap was rapidly wearing away, necessitating the relocation of the lighthouse to the mainland.

The threat posed by the eroding rock must not have been too great as the tower was altered to receive a new lantern, lighting apparatus, and revolving machinery delivered to the station on August 4, 1875. A temporary fixed white light was displayed until the new revolving light went into service on October 18, 1875. In 1877, a frame tower was built near the lighthouse to support a fog bell, which was struck every twelve seconds, when needed.

It was fire, not erosion, which eventually claimed Quaco Lighthouse. On June 17, 1881, a fire broke out in a defective flue between the ceiling and the roof of the keeper's dwelling and destroyed all the buildings at the station. A temporary pole light was erected on the nearby headland known as West Head and placed in operation on July 9. Five acres on West Head were acquired for $200, and a contract for a new lighthouse was awarded to D. W. Clark at $2,890.

The second lighthouse stood 366 metres from the site of the previous one and consisted of a square, pyramidal tower and an attached keeper's dwelling. Its white revolving light was displayed for the first time on April 20, 1883. Keeper Love retired in 1884, and was replaced by Charles Brown. That same year, a landing block was constructed at the station to facilitate the receiving of supplies.

An iron bell buoy was moored in eighteen metres of water off the headland in 1886, and a $970 contract was awarded that year for the construction of a fog alarm building. This structure was completed the following year, and a steam-powered foghorn was placed in operation on September 1, 1887. Lorenzo B. Bradshaw was

Travel Instructions: From Highway 1, east of Saint John, take Exit 137A and follow Route 111 toward St. Martins for 38 kilometres. Just before St. Martins, turn right onto West Quaco Road, drive 1.8 kilometres, and then turn left onto Lighthouse Road and drive 1.2 kilometres to reach the lighthouse.

Established: 1835 (present tower 1966)

Position: 45.32369 N, -65.53578 W

Light: White, on 0.3 s, eclipse 9.7 s

Tower Height: 11.6 metres

Focal Plane: 26 metres

Description: White rectangular tower rising from corner of one-storey white building, red lantern

hired as the fog alarm engineer, but a new six-room dwelling for the engineer was not completed until 1906.

On January 28, 1885, during a blinding snowstorm the American schooner *Arcana* ran aground off Quaco Head with a crew of ten. Four men were lost without a trace, while five died of exposure clinging to the rocks awaiting rescue. The tenth crewmember managed to drag himself up the cliff to the safety of the lighthouse. There is a monument to the crew in the nearby Quaco Cemetery.

The present Quaco Head Lighthouse was constructed in 1966, and the station was de-staffed in 1987.

39. St. Martins Visitor Information Centre

Topped by the lantern from the 1883 Quaco Head Lighthouse, this picturesque faux tower serves as a visitor information centre in St. Martins.

Travel Instructions: If travelling on Route 111 from either Saint John or Sussex, take Main Street into St. Martins and you will find the lighthouse near the harbour.

Established: 1983

Position: 45.35970 N, -65.53262 W

Light: Inactive

Tower Height: 8 metres

Description: White square pyramidal tower, red lantern

Work on this faux lighthouse began in 1983 as a community bicentennial project, and when it was completed the following year it was topped by the lantern room from the 1883 Quaco Head Lighthouse and opened as the St. Martins visitor information centre. Visitors can climb to the lantern for a 360° view of the harbour and two nearby historic covered bridges.

40. St. Martins Breakwater

On December 1, 1887, a fixed red light was shown for the first time from a 6.4-metre-high, square tower positioned on the outer end of the eastern breakwater pier at St. Martins. James Cochran was appointed the first keeper of the light, which served to guide vessels into the inner harbour.

A violent storm struck St. Martins on February 1, 1908, and swept away the tower and the outer 18.3 metres of the breakwater. A temporary mast light was immediately erected and served until 1910, when a new, 6.7-metre tower was erected on the east breakwater extension. This replacement tower was destroyed by a storm in December of 1917. A pole light was subsequently erected on the west breakwater, and a triangular, skeletal tower was supporting a light on the east breakwater in 2011.

Two different towers served at this location over a period of thirty years; the second for only seven years. It is unknown which of the two towers is seen here. (Library and Archives Canada)

Lupins and the Bayswater Lighthouse, both found along the roadside on the Kingston Peninsula.

ST. JOHN RIVER

In 1816, the *General Smythe*, named for New Brunswick's second imperial governor, became the first steamboat to offer passenger service on the St. John River. Travelling at eight kilometers per hour, journeys between Saint John and Fredericton initially took a full day, but faster steamers cut the travel time in half by the 1860s.

Provincial wharves were built, followed later by federal wharves, and the St. John River became the main artery for goods and passengers in southern New Brunswick. Grand resorts sprung up along the shores of the river to the delight of travellers.

As steamboat traffic increased, beacons were needed to mark the river. Precedence dictated that construction and maintenance of lighthouses be paid for by a duty levied on vessels that benefited from them, so a bill to collect light duties from the riverboats was prepared in 1848. This legislation did not pass, and the St. John River remained dark for two more decades.

Finally, on August 20, 1869, two years after Confederation, the department of marine established six beacon lights located from south to north along the river at Swift Point, Sand Point, Oak Point, No Man's Friend, Oromocto Shoals, and Wilmot Bluff. For $1,044, John Duffy erected all six lights, which were rather crude, consisting of a lantern on a mast or a lantern on a mast atop an open framework. The total cost for the lights, including construction, superintendence, and lighting apparatuses, was $2,342, and another $600 was spent to acquire the sites. The original six lighthouses were later replaced by enclosed structures.

Unlike the larger coastal lights, the keepers along the river did not live at the lights but rather within an easy walking distance. Many points along the St. John River and its tributaries are named after the early owners of the land, and as lighthouses were built on these points, it was only natural that the landowners, in many cases the only residents living near the site, became the first lightkeepers. This was the case at Belyeas Point, McColgan Point, Robertson Point, Cox Point, Fanjoys Point, Bridges Point, and Palmer's Landing. Keepers were not only responsible for the twice-daily duties of the light but also for the maintenance and upkeep of the towers.

Introduction of train service and the advent of the automobile doomed steamboat service, and the last run was made in 1946. The wharves that served the riverboats fell into disrepair, and the grand hotels all but disappeared. Today, twelve lighthouses remain standing as reminders of that period.

41. Swift Point (Green Head)

Swift Point Lighthouse with a view of the lower portion of the St. John River.

Travel Instructions: From Route 1 at Catherwood, take Exit 119 and travel north along Catherwood Street to Manawagonish Road. Turn right onto Manawagonish Road, and at the first traffic signal make a left onto Church Avenue and then make a quick right onto Green Head Road. Continue on this road then make a right turn onto Quarry Road, which will loop back onto Green Head Road. A little over midway along this loop, look for a gated dirt road on your right, where you need to park and begin your hike. It is just over one kilometre to the lighthouse.

Established: 1869 (present tower 1896)

Position: 45.28242 N, -66.12133 W

Light: Green, on 2 s, eclipse 10 s

Tower Height: 13.9 metres

Focal Plane: 28.1 metres

Description: White square pyramidal tower, red lantern

Swift Point Light was placed in operation on August 20, 1869, with John Nelson Williams as its first keeper. In 1872, the lantern caught fire and forced the suspension of the light for a few nights.

The department of marine report for 1892 noted that the "skeleton lighthouse" at Green Head was in bad order and tenders would be invited during the coming winter for a new enclosed tower. A replacement was not built until 1896, as noted in that year's report:

A new lighthouse has been erected at Green Head, 24 feet east of the site formerly occupied by the old light on a mast, which is now discontinued. The lighthouse is a white, square wooden building 50 feet high, situated 105 feet above high water mark. The illuminating apparatus is dioptric, the light being fixed white, elevated 150 feet above the surface of the water and visible 10 miles from all points of approach by water. The work was done under contract by Mr. G. W. Palmer, the lowest bidder, his contract price being $579.

In 1900, Keeper Thomas E. Looney was supplied with a hand foghorn to be sounded when the fog signals of vessels were heard. A mechanical fog bell replaced the hand foghorn in 1914. A Cunningham air whistle was installed in 1964, much to the consternation of the residents in the area. Complaints led to the installation of a fog bell striker a year later.

Swift Point Lighthouse works in tandem with Sand Point Lighthouse to help vessels navigate the lower portion of the St. John River and locate the narrow entrance to the Reversing Falls section, an area of often confusing tributaries, bays, and islands.

42. McColgan Point

McColgan Point Lighthouse in 2011, with Kennebecasis Island in the background.

McColgan Point Lighthouse was constructed in 1913 to guide vessels between Kennebecasis Island and the Kingston Peninsula. The tower was originally equipped with a sixth-order dioptric lens, and Samuel McColgan served as the first keeper of the light.

In September of 1956 the local community requested a fog bell to aid the nearby ferry. A Cunningham air whistle was installed in May of 1957 and put forth a blast of 2.5 seconds followed by 27.5 seconds of silence.

Kenneth Wilson was appointed keeper on June 1, 1967, at an annual salary of $690. He served until full automation on December 1, 1969.

Travel Instructions: At the lower end of the Kingston Peninsula where Route 845 makes a ninety-degree turn, continue straight following the sign toward the Peninsula Princess ferry. Follow this road straight to its terminus at the Kennebecasis Island ferry. The lighthouse is visible from the nearby shore or from the ferry.

Established: 1913

Position: 45.33222 N, -66.10956 W

Light: White, on 2 s, eclipse 10 s

Tower Height: 8.2 metres

Focal Plane: 11.3 metres

Description: White square pyramidal tower, red-roofed lantern

43. Bayswater

Freshly painted Bayswater Lighthouse, 2011.

Travel Instructions: Located adjacent to Route 845 in the community of Bayswater on the Kingston Peninsula, just west of a historic covered bridge.

Established: 1913

Position: 45.35055 N, -66.13336 W

Light: Inactive since 2005

Tower Height: 8.2 metres

Focal Plane: 10.4 metres

Description: White square pyramidal tower, red-roofed lantern

Bayswater Lighthouse and McColgan Point Lighthouse, separated by just 2.8 kilometres, were both built in 1913 by B. R. Palmer of Tennant's Cove. The towers are nearly identical, but the contract price for Bayswater was $825, while McColgan Point was built for $700.

Bayswater Lighthouse was deactivated in 2005. In 2010 a local group was given a two-year lease on the lighthouse with the assumption that it would be turned over to them afterward.

44. Sand Point

The first keeper of Sand Point Light, J. Cauldfield, was hired in 1869 and received the same salary as the other five original St. John River lightkeepers: eighty dollars.

A new Sand Point Lighthouse, the tallest on the St. John River, was completed in 1898 and described in that year's *Annual Report of the Department of Marine*:

> *The mast on an open framework, from which the light was shown at Sand Point, on the River St. John, has been removed and replaced by a square skeletal framed steel tower, with sloping sides, surmounted by an enclosed wooden light room and by a square wooden lantern.*
>
> *The new lighthouse stands on the site of the old mast, about 150 feet back from high water mark, on the most prominent part of the point. The lantern and iron-work are painted red, and the enclosed upper part of the tower is painted white. The height of the building, from the base to the ventilator on the lantern is 58 feet.*
>
> *The light shown from the new building is a seventh order dioptric, fixed white light, elevated 60 feet above high water mark, and should be visible 13 miles from all points of approach by water.*
>
> *The work was done by Mr. G. W. Palmer, [of] Kars, his contract price being $699.*

On June 30, 1959, a Notice to Mariners went out declaring Sand Point to be an unwatched light, changed from fixed white to fixed red.

Many of the lighthouses along the St. John River were built on or adjacent to wharves, like the Sand Point Lighthouse located at the lower end of the Kingston Peninsula.

Travel Instructions: From Route 845 on the lower end of the Kingston Peninsula, take Sand Point Wharf Road south to its terminus at the lighthouse. The wharf and property near the lighthouse are private.

Established: 1869 (present tower 1898)

Position: 45.342611 N, -66.19883 W

Light: Fixed red

Tower Height: 17.7 metres

Focal Plane: 22.7 metres

Description: Red skeletal tower with white enclosed upper portion, red lantern

45. Belyeas Point

This area is prone to flooding during the spring freshet, often making the Belyeas Point Lighthouse appear to be floating in the river until the water recedes.

Travel Instructions: Take Exit 80 from Route 7 and travel north through the flashing light onto Route 102 for approximately 3.2 kilometres. In the community of Morrisdale, make a right on Lighthouse Lane and drive down the hill. The lighthouse is easily viewed from the cul-de-sac.

Established: 1882 (present tower 1930s)

Position: 45.37817 N, -66.21606 W

Light: Green, on 1 s, eclipse 4 s

Tower Height: 11.9 metres

Focal Plane: 12.7 metres

Description: White square pyramidal tower, red lantern

In 1881, Parliament appropriated $800 for Belyeas Point Lighthouse. Tenders were subsequently called for, and a $395 construction contract was awarded to Saunders Clark of Carleton.

The lighthouse commenced operation on June 1, 1882, with Spafford Barker Belyea serving as keeper at an annual salary of eighty dollars. The *Annual Report of the Department of Marine* for that year described the lighthouse:

> *The light is fixed white with an illuminating dioptric apparatus of the 6th order; is elevated 40 feet above water mark and should be visible 11 miles from all points of approach. The tower, which stands upon a small timber crib, is a square wooden building painted white, and 36 feet high from the pier to the vane on the lantern. The lighthouse is situated on the extreme point near the water's edge, on the west side of the river, and the light is for the purpose of guiding vessels clear of Purdy's Shoal on the opposite side of the river, and for the general purposes of navigation.*

Severe flooding damaged the original lighthouse in the 1930s, leading to the tower being rebuilt and moved inland. Even resting atop pylons on more elevated terrain, the new Belyeas Point Lighthouse has been damaged by the spring freshet several times over the years.

46. Glenwood

In 1911, a mast light, with a shed at its base, was established on the west side of the St. John River on Belyea's wharf, later known as Glenwood. It displayed a fixed white light from a seventh-order lens lantern. H. Belyea was appointed the first keeper but served less than one year. The mast and shed were destroyed in March of 1936 during the spring freshet and replaced later that year by a square, tapered wooden lighthouse. This lighthouse lasted less than ten years and was likely destroyed in the same manner as its predecessor.

Today the wharf is privately owned and is a popular gathering spot for pleasure crafts.

Glenwood Lighthouse, 1936. (Canadian Coast Guard)

47. The Cedars

Starting in 1884, a lamp shown from a mast was exhibited at Williams Landing on the eastern shore of the St. John River. This light was discontinued in 1904, when a square, wooden tower went into service at the Cedars, located just 1.2 kilometres upstream.

Forrest W. Williams, who had been in charge of the light at Williams Landing, was the first keeper of the Cedars Lighthouse, which originally employed a seventh-order lens in its lantern room to produce a fixed white light.

In 1894 a large summer hotel had opened in the community of Long Reach in a sub-community known as the Cedars, after the large cedar trees gracing the nearby shores of the St. John River. The hotel became a destination for folks who wanted a day, a week, or a season to relax in the country along the banks of the beautiful river.

The Cedars Lighthouse in 1998, two years after being decommissioned.

James E. Ganong was appointed keeper of the Cedars Lighthouse in 1912, after Forrest Williams was dismissed for being an "aggressive member of the liberal party." In his application, Keeper Ganong listed his birth year as 1874 and his age as thirty-eight. The application also included a signed statement by a magistrate attesting that Ganong was of good moral character, able to read and write, and had a fair knowledge of arithmetic. This first quality would later be called into question.

In October 1920, Keeper Ganong, who was supposedly just forty-six, received a letter informing him that due to his "advancing age" his department had recommended him for retirement. There had been some uncertainty regarding his age, but John Kelly, superintendent of lights in New Brunswick, said despite what he claimed on his application, Keeper Ganong had told him that he was born in 1847. In an interdepartmental letter, Kelly wrote, "Mr. Ganong appears to be a very old man, and is very feeble, and I do not think will be able to carry on his duties much longer."

Despite being in reality seventy-three years of age, Keeper Ganong appealed his proposed retirement on the grounds of "good health, efficiency and continued ability to perform" his duties. Keeper Ganong's good health didn't last much longer, as he suffered a paralytic stroke in January of 1921 while visiting his son near Boston. Amazingly, James Ganong would remain the official keeper of the Cedars Lighthouse until 1923, though his son Walter started looking after the light with the opening of navigation in the spring of 1921.

In June 1923, John Kelly provided the marine department with an update on Keeper Ganong: "I beg to state there is not much change in Mr. Ganong's condition. He has not resigned, nor is he leaving the county. He is a very sick man, is in the County Hospital, and I believe is only a matter of a short time before he will improve or die."

Keeper Ganong passed away on August 14, 1923. M. J. Doney, who was renting Keeper Ganong's farm, had been looking after the light and continued to do so until September 15, when Frank Gorham was appointed keeper. A gratuity of twenty-five dollars was divided amongst Keeper Ganong's two sons and the widow of his third son.

Frank Gorham minded the light until late 1930, when he fell victim to political wrangling and was dismissed on charges of active political partisanship. Thomas Bissett, who lived "within a stones throw of the Cedars Light," was appointed keeper in his stead. Clotillie May Bissett became the first female keeper of record for the lighthouse when her husband passed away in June 1932. Starting at a salary of $150 per year, Mrs. Bissett served as keeper for four years.

On September 18, 1958, the Cedars Lighthouse was electrified and changed from fixed white to fixed red.

The Cedars was decommissioned in 1996, and that same year Peninsula Heritage began its efforts to acquire the tower from the federal government. It took nine years, but in 2005 the lighthouse was finally turned over to the organization. A trail to the lighthouse was opened in 2008 making the secluded lighthouse accessible to the public by land.

Travel Instructions: On the west side of the Kingston Peninsula, take Route 845 to the community of Long Reach. Approximately 1 kilometre north of Williams Road, you will see Frances Smith Memorial Hall on the east side of Route 845 and St. James Church on the west side. Directly across from the hall, a small footpath leads 0.3 kilometres to the lighthouse. There is no public access to drive to the lighthouse.

Established: 1904

Position: 45.47843 N, -66.08271 W

Light: Inactive since 1994

Tower Height: 10 metres

Focal Plane: 13.4 metres

Description: White square pyramidal tower, red lantern

48. Oak Point

The active Oak Point Lighthouse is one of six lights established in 1869 and is one of only two hazard lights found along the St. John River.

Travel Instructions: From Route 102 on the west side of the St. John River, make a right turn at the sign for Oak Point Provincial Park. A park entrance fee is charged from mid-May through Labour Day.

Established: 1869 (present tower 1902)

Position: 45.50752 N, -66.080009 W

Light: Green, on 2 s, eclipse 8 s

Tower Height: 14.1 metres

Focal Plane: 15.5 metres

Description: White square pyramidal tower, red lantern

Situated at the northern end of the Reach, a wide, straight section of the St. John River that runs along the west side of the Kingston Peninsula, Oak Point was home to one of the original six river lights established in 1869.

The current Oak Point Lighthouse was constructed in 1902, and a detailed description of this structure is found in that year's *Annual Report of the Department of Marine:*

The light shown from a lantern on a mast on Oak point, river St. John, has been replaced by a stronger light shown from an inclosed [sic] lighthouse tower, built 56 feet outside the site of the old light, on the shore on the east extremity of the point. The light shown from the new tower is fixed white dioptric, elevated 49 feet above high water mark, and visible 12 miles from all points of approach.

The lighthouse is a square wooden building with sloping sides, painted white, surmounted by a square wooden lantern painted red. The height of the building from its base to the ventilator on the lantern is 48 feet. The old mast and shed have been taken down.

The Kiwanis Club that operates Oak Point Campground had a lease on the lighthouse for several years in the late 1990s. A deck and stairs were built on the landward side of the tower, and for a couple of years, the lighthouse served as a gift shop. In 2001, the club installed a window on the ground floor of the tower, facing the river, with plans to use the lighthouse for overnight rentals. When the Coast Guard learned of the alterations, the lease was revoked, the deck and stairs torn down, and the window removed and boarded up.

49. Shamper's Wharf

Shamper's Wharf Lighthouse, 1928. (Canadian Coast Guard)

B. R. Palmer built Shamper's Wharf Lighthouse in 1913 for $1,049. Located atop a bluff near the entrance to Belleisle Bay, the tower employed a sixth-order lens to beam forth a fixed white light. The light was discontinued in 1961 and sold to a private owner. After standing neglected for years, the tower was burned to the ground in 2000.

50. Palmer's Landing

Palmer's Landing Lighthouse, 1936. (Canadian Coast Guard)

In 1884, a beacon light was established on Palmer's Landing, just north of the entrance to Belleisle Bay. Beverley Emerson Palmer was appointed first keeper and was still responsible for the light in 1895, when a spark from the steamer *Hampstead* set fire to the wharf and destroyed the light.

A square, wooden lighthouse, built on the new government high-water wharf, commenced operation on August 6, 1896. By 1961 the wharf had settled, causing the lighthouse to lean. Repairing it was deemed too expensive, so a pole light was erected on the adjacent low-water wharf, and in December 1961 the old lighthouse was burned. In 1965, the light was returned to the high-water wharf. Today only crumbling remains of these wharves mark the location.

51. Hampstead Wharf

Hampstead Wharf Lighthouse on its original cribwork, 1989. (Canadian Coast Guard)

Hampstead Wharf Lighthouse and informational sign on lighthouses of the St. John River, 2011.

On October 29, 1900, a lens lantern, hoisted up a 9.4-metre mast, commenced operation on the public wharf at Hampstead, located on the western shore of the St. John River, north of Belleisle Bay and south of Washademoak Lake. A 6.4-metre-tall square wooden tower, placed atop wooden cribwork on the south side of the low-water wharf, replaced the mast light in 1912.

Hampstead Light was deactivated in 1994, and in 1999 the Coast Guard determined that its supporting cribwork was unstable. The tower was accordingly relocated to the high-water wharf, where it was chained in place with its lantern boarded up. The St. John River Society relocated the tower to higher ground behind the wharf in 2001. After acquiring the lighthouse in 2009, the society restored and painted it in 2010.

Travel Instructions: From Route 102 in the community of Hampstead, take the turnoff for the former Hampstead ferry. Hampstead Lighthouse is located alongside the road near the wharf.

Established: 1900 (present tower 1912)

Position: 45.62522 N, -66.08452 W

Light: Inactive since 1994

Tower Height: 5.5 metres

Description: White square tower, red-roofed lantern

52. Lower Musquash Island
53. Hendry Farm

The Lower Musquash Island Lighthouse is only visible from the water. Decommissioned in 1994, its only visitors now are grazing cattle.

The decommissioned Hendry Farm Lighthouse was acquired by the Village of Cambridge Narrows in 2005.

In 1874, Parliament appropriated money for range lights to mark the entrance to Washademoak Lake. One tower was placed on the east side of Lower Musquash Island, an irregularly shaped island that encloses a large freshwater lagoon and guards the entrance to the lake, and the other at Hendry Farm, near Central Cambridge.

The range lights, which consisted of open framework towers, painted brown and topped with white lanterns, were put into operation on April 1, 1876. Daniel Smith was the first keeper of Lower Musquash Island Light, while Joseph Hendry was the first to tend Hendry Farm Light.

An 1878 *List of Lights* provided the following instructions for using the lights:

In coming down the lake, the two lights to be kept in range until opposite the N.W. end of Hog Island, whence a southerly course to be kept to the foot of Musquash Island.

In going up the lake, the two lights to be brought in range opposite the N.W. end of Hog Island, and kept in range until within half a mile of the light on Hendry Farm.

In 1893, the dilapidated original lights were replaced with new towers. Sixth-order dioptric lenses were installed in the towers in 1909, replacing catoptric apparatuses.

Lower Musquash Island Lighthouse was discontinued in 1922, but then re-established two years later at the opening of navigation in 1924.

Elisha Melvin Hendry, who owned the farm surrounding the light, served as keeper from 1880 to 1888 and again from 1897 until his death in 1899. Melvin's daughter Annie Melissa was appointed keeper in his place and served until 1923, when she married. Mary, a second daughter, then took charge of the light for three years until her own marriage.

Lower Musquash Island Lighthouse was decommissioned in 1994, and Hendry Farm Lighthouse was discontinued the following year. In September 2005, Senator Joseph Day participated in a ceremony marking the official transfer of Hendry Farm Lighthouse to the Village of Cambridge-Narrows.

Lower Musquash Island

Travel Instructions: Lower Musquash Island Lighthouse is best viewed by boat.

Established: 1876 (present tower 1893)

Position: 45.70780 N, -66.06639 W

Light: Inactive since 1994

Tower Height: 12 metres

Focal Plane: 12.2 metres

Description: White square pyramidal tower atop red timbers, red lantern

Hendry Farm

Travel Instructions: From Route 715, between Central and Lower Cambridge take Hendry Farm Road, which ends at Washademoak Lane. The lighthouse is located down Washademoak Lane on the right.

Established: 1876 (present tower 1893)

Position: 45.73275 N, -66.04842 W

Light: Inactive since 1995

Tower Height: 8 metres

Focal Plane: 9.1 metres

Description: White square pyramidal tower, red lantern

54. Gagetown

As part of the St. John River Campaign (1758–59), Colonel Robert Monckton led a force of British soldiers on a mission to destroy Acadian settlements. Fifty Acadian families who had settled along the St. John River near the Village of Gagetown were forced to abandon their homes. Gagetown subsequently became a Loyalist community, and in the late 1800s and early 1900s, was a stop for riverboats.

Gagetown received its first lighthouse in 1895, when a square, pyramidal tower, surmounted by a square lantern, was erected atop a cribwork pier. The wooden tower, which stood 14.3 metres tall, was white with a red lantern. The tower's fixed white light was intended to mark the nearby dramatic turn in the river.

This peculiarly sharp bend was known as "No Man's Friend," as sailing vessels were forced to tack

The original tower before it was destroyed by ice in 1934. (Canadian Coast Guard)

View of Gagetown Lighthouse from the Gagetown cable ferry.

laboriously. No Man's Friend was the site of one of the six original beacon lights placed along the river in 1869, but by 1894, the tower was much decayed, and it was replaced by Gagetown Lighthouse, built on the opposite shore of the river.

On April 10, 1901, the spring freshet carried away Gagetown Lighthouse. As a temporary measure, a fixed white light was shown from a lantern suspended from a nearby elm tree until the lighthouse was retrieved, put back in place, and relit on June 22.

Gagetown Lighthouse was destroyed by ice in April 1934, and a replacement tower, the one that remains today, was completed by G. N. Breen four months later. The current design, with its open supportive stilts, has helped lengthen the lifespan of the lighthouse.

The tower's square lantern room is still equipped with a Chance Brothers seventh-order drum dioptric which includes a matching green glass liner.

55. *Jemseg*

In 1884, a mast light was built upon a timber pier to guide vessels navigating the St. John River through the channel at the entrance to the Jemseg River. George Nevers was the first keeper responsible for hoisting the lantern, containing a fixed red light, to the top of the 6.4-metre mast.

A unique latticework tower later replaced the mast light.

Jemseg Lighthouse, 1938. (Canadian Coast Guard)

56. Robertson Point
57. Fanjoys Point

Robertson Point Lighthouse, 1925. (Library and Archives Canada)

Fanjoys Point Lighthouse, 1970s. (Canadian Coast Guard)

Grand Lake, the largest freshwater lake in New Brunswick, drains into the St. John River through the 6.7-kilometre-long Jemseg River. After six lights were established along the St. John River in 1869, the next three lights to be erected in the St. John River watershed were along the shores of Grand Lake. After a light was commissioned at Cox Point in 1871, Charles Macpherson constructed 4.9-metre-tall towers at Fanjoys Point and Robertson Point on the southwestern shore of the lake in 1873.

John Robertson and William Fanjoy started serving as keepers of their namesake lights on October 1, 1873. Both lights were improved in 1905, when a single lamp and a seventh-order lens replaced the antiquated lamps and reflectors.

Cylindrical towers topped by exposed lights replaced the attractive wooden lighthouses in 1964. These modern navigational aids were still active in 2011.

58. Cox Point

In 1869, $650 was allocated to construct Grand Lake's first lighthouse, and the resulting Cox Point Lighthouse commenced operation on May 3, 1871, with Michael J. Cox, owner of the surrounding land, receiving an annual salary of $80 to serve as keeper. After two years of service, the lighthouse was equipped with additional bracing and another window on its south side to guide vessels into Cumberland Bay.

Due to its exposed location, Cox Point Lighthouse was often struck by ice floes during the spring freshet. In 1888, the freshet tore the tower from the point, but it was quickly replaced and put in good order. When the tower was toppled again the following year, the department of marine raised the protective wall around the tower.

The lighthouse employed lamps and reflectors until 1905, when a seventh-order lens was installed.

Micah Y. Cox was appointed keeper at Cox Point in 1875 and served until his passing in 1892. As was customary, the department of marine gave the keeper's widow, Eliza, a gratuity of two months of her husband's salary, and as no one else lived near the point, they also placed her in temporary charge of the light.

Eliza was still tending the light in 1897 when Walter Butler sent a letter to a government official expressing his view that as the Liberals were now in charge, a conservative such as Eliza Cox shouldn't have a government job. "A woman is not eligible for a lightkeeper, I believe at any rate," Butler wrote, "and there are some life long liberals living near who expected, and it was expected by the Liberal leaders here, that one of them would be appointed."

Butler anticipated that removing a widow from the position might be frowned upon, so he explained that Eliza was not a "poor widow," but rather was "flourishing like a green bay tree." Butler asserted that "by some sort of chicanery" Eliza had "retained her deceased husband's rather fine property, and paid none of his debts."

There was indeed some reluctance to remove Eliza, but when she married later in 1897, the deputy minister of marine and fisheries informed her that her "temporary" appointment was being cancelled since she had remarried. Eliza was told to turn charge of the light over to William Barton, who had been recommended by Walter Butler.

Eliza's new husband, Alexander McBaine, wrote to the deputy minister expressing a desire to be appointed keeper. McBaine explained that he owned the land on which the lighthouse stood and was as good a Liberal as Barton, who lived over three kilometres from the light and could never reach it during the spring freshet.

When William Barton showed up to take charge of the light, Eliza refused to relinquish control or to allow Barton to pass over her land to reach the light, as the government had no right-of-way.

The 1917 concrete tower as it appeared in 1935. (Canadian Coast Guard)

In a letter to the minister of marine and fisheries dated April 5, 1898, Keeper Barton agreed to resign, citing that it was "inconvenient for anyone to attend the light except those that live on the farm." Alexander McBaine kept the light for at least twenty years, and during his service, a reinforced concrete tower was built at Cox Point in 1917 at a cost of $985. This tower served until 1966, and a triangular skeletal tower marked the point in 2011.

59. McMann Point

McMann Point Lighthouse, 1925.
(Canadian Coast Guard)

A square wooden tower, painted white and standing 7.9 metres tall, was placed at McMann Point in 1876. Built by C. McPherson, the lighthouse was the fourth to be established on Grand Lake and directed marine traffic at Newcastle, near the northern end of the lake. The tower's fixed white light, produced by a lamp and reflector, commenced operation on November 1, 1876. The light had been discontinued by 1947.

60. Bridges Point

Bridges Point Lighthouse, 1933. (Canadian Coast Guard)

In 1891, Frederick W. Bailey constructed Bridges Point Lighthouse for $439 on land near Sheffield purchased from Mary A. Bridges for $150. The lighthouse, a square, pyramidal tower, painted white with a red lantern roof, stood atop a square cribwork block and measured 9.1 metres tall. Abraham Bridges was appointed first keeper of the light at an annual salary of $80.

During an inspection in 1893, it was reported that the tower was too short and had been poorly placed. Two years later, the lighthouse was moved sixty-one metres north, closer to the water's edge, where it could be better seen both up and down the river. This tower served until 1957, and its successor, a pole light, was discontinued in 1965.

61. Oromocto Shoals

The 1895 tower sometime before it was lost to arson in 1962. (Canadian Coast Guard)

Oromocto Shoals consisted of a series of bars that stretched across the St. John River just below Fredericton. In 1855, a dredge cut a channel through the principal bar, and a light was built to guide vessels through this hazardous stretch in 1869.

Around 1878, this light was relocated to the outer end of a recently built wharf, where it served until its skeletal frame was so rotten that it had to be replaced. In 1895, a new enclosed lighthouse was built southeast of the light's former location. This square, pyramidal tower started displaying a fixed white light from its seventh-order lens on October 1, 1895. Perched atop a cribwork pier, the tower was 14.3 metres tall and was painted white, except for its red lantern.

This attractive tower, after being vandalized on more than one occasion, burned to the ground on May 11, 1962, and was never replaced.

62. Wilmot Bluff

When New Brunswick became a separate colony from Nova Scotia in 1784, Ste. Anne's Point, which had just been settled by Loyalists the previous year, was named the capital, largely due to its central inland location that made it less prone to an American attack. In 1785, a street plan was laid out west of Ste. Anne's Point, and this new site, named "Frederick's Town," in honour of Prince Frederick Augustus, the second son of King George III, was made the capital.

On August 20, 1869, a light at Wilmot Bluff just below Fredericton was put in operation, and J. D. Wilmot, who owned the surrounding property, was appointed first keeper. A lantern hoisted atop a mast was used to produce a white light at a focal plane of 31.7

metres above high-water mark. The light was partially destroyed by fire in 1882, but it was thoroughly repaired and placed back in operation.

In 1908 Wilmot Bluff became the last of the original six lights to be replaced by an enclosed tower. John C. Palmer was awarded a $1,060 contract to construct the new lighthouse—a square tower, with sloping sides, surmounted by a square, wooden lantern. The 12.8-metre-tall lighthouse originally stood on a cribwork foundation.

When the lighthouse was decommissioned in 1967, its last keeper, Clarence Gillies, expressed interest in purchasing the tower but didn't want to relocate it or reduce its height, which was a requirement imposed by

Wilmot Bluff Lighthouse, 1933. (Canadian Coast Guard)

Privately owned Wilmot Bluff Lighthouse, 2011.

the government so the tower couldn't be seen from the river.

In June of 1969, the lighthouse was instead sold for $604 to Gillies's son-in-law, B. Napier Simpson, who planned to cut it into three sections and move it to Ontario. This plan proved too costly, and after six months the government threatened legal action.

Mrs. Gillies, whose husband Clarence had passed away by this time, was very upset by the thought of the lighthouse being demolished or blemished, so the government agreed to let the lighthouse remain where it was. Simpson signed ownership of the tower over to his mother-in-law, who in turn signed it over to her son, Gerald Gillies. In February of 1970, the superintendent of lights inspected the property and agreed that Gerald Gillies could keep the lighthouse intact at its original location if it were maintained in good condition

Travel Instructions: Take the Nevers Road Exit (297) off the Trans-Canada Highway and go north on Nevers Road until it ends at Route 102. Make a right onto Route 102 and continue past the Fredericton Airport. When the road makes a sharp 90° curve to the right, continue straight ahead on Thatch Road, where you will find the tower on your left. The lighthouse is on private property but can be viewed from the top of the driveway.

Established: 1869 (present tower 1908)

Position: 45.86919 N, -66.51047 W

Light: Inactive

Tower Height: 13 metres

Focal Plane: 30.5 metres

Description: White square pyramidal tower, red lantern

Martin Head Lighthouse, 1927. (Library and Archives Canada)

CHIGNECTO BAY AND TRIBUTARIES

63. Martin Head

Martin Head is a small hill, which marks the western side of the entrance to Chignecto Bay and is connected to the mainland by a narrow causeway. Thomas B. Carson began construction of a fog alarm building and dwelling on Martin Head in 1884, and the signal commenced operation in 1885, with George Adie Briggs as its first engineer. Four years later, the signal was discontinued and relocated across Chignecto Bay to Apple River, Nova Scotia.

In 1914, Martin Head received a navigational aid of a different sort when F. H. Carson built a square, wooden dwelling with an octagonal lantern centred on its hipped roof on the former site of the fog alarm. The lighthouse had a height of 11.6 metres, but, due to Martin Head, the light's fourth-order lens had a lofty focal plane of 41.8 metres. Martin Head Lighthouse was discontinued in 1963.

64. Cape Enrage

Cape Enrage is the southern tip of Barn Marsh Island, which is separated from the mainland by an easily passable, narrow tidal creek. The cape was named for a reef that extends seaward from the point and causes the surrounding waters to become violent or enraged during maximum tidal currents.

A petition from merchants and ship owners of Westmorland County for a lighthouse on Cape Enrage was presented to the government of New Brunswick in 1837, and in response the legislature appropriated a sum not exceeding £600 for the project.

When the commissioners of lighthouses for the Bay of Fundy initiated site selection at Cape Enrage, they quickly discovered that interested parties were sharply divided over whether a lighthouse on Cape Enrage was preferable to one situated across Chignecto Bay at Apple River, Nova Scotia. Written opinions from "the most experienced coasters" were solicited, and three gentlemen submitted letters in support of Apple River, with one boldly claiming "a light at Apple River will be of a thousand times more benefit to the public than one at Cape Enrage."

Only one letter favouring Cape Enrage was received, but it carried thirty-three signatures. These mariners submitted four reasons why Cape Enrage was the preferred location:

1. As Cape Enrage extended over a third of the way across Chignecto Bay, it was a serious hazard.

2. A rocky spur extended outward from the cape another kilometre, making it still more dangerous.

3. The water off the cape was deep, making soundings of no use, while soundings could be used at Apple River to determine one's proximity to the shore.

4. The shore around Cape Enrage was ice-free in winter, while the south shore was often blocked.

The commissioners decided in favour of Cape Enrage but suggested that the Lieutenant-Governor notify his counterpart in Nova Scotia that a light at Apple River would greatly aid those navigating the bay.

The site for Cape Enrage Lighthouse was purchased from Daniel Tingley, who offered to sell five acres on the extreme point of the cape for £20 and grant a right-of-way across his property. Rather than purchase a lantern for Cape Enrage, the commissioners ordered a new lantern from England for Partridge Island and transferred its lantern to Cape Enrage. The English lantern arrived late, delaying the activation of Cape Enrage Lighthouse until the spring of 1840. The first keeper, James Munson, was paid £18 for living in and taking care of the lighthouse for part of 1839 but did not receive his full pay until the light was activated.

Although Cape Enrage Lighthouse was the eighth to be constructed in New Brunswick, it was the first square tower, all of the preceding being octagonal. Keeper Munson and his family lived in the 11.9-metre-tall lighthouse, which employed six lamps and reflectors to produce a fixed white light.

In 1845, £50 was allocated to construct a road to the lighthouse, and in 1849, a landing was built on the east side of the cape, and stairs and skids were put in place so the station could more easily be supplied from the bay.

Today the 1952 keeper's duplex at Cape Enrage is known as Cape House and serves as a dormitory and popular café.

In 1868, the lighthouse was declared worn out, and work on a new tower was completed the following year. The new light, however, was not exhibited until November 16, 1870, due to delays in receiving the lighting apparatus, a fourth-order lens. The old lighthouse, minus its lantern room, continued to be used as the keeper's residence.

A fog alarm building was completed at Cape Enrage in 1874, and an old boiler and engine from Partridge Island were installed therein. The whistle commenced operation on October 20 of that year and was cared for by William J. Starratt, who had been placed in charge of the station just a week before. Keeper Starratt received an annual salary of eight hundred dollars, out of which he hired an engineer to run the fog alarm. A new dwelling was also constructed in 1874 to house the keeper and engineer, along with their families. Marine agent John H. Harding noted the benefit provided by the new fog alarm: "The dread which this Cape and its frightful ledges have excited in the past has now given place to a feeling of confidence and security."

In 1876, lightning struck the lighthouse, just below the lantern floor, and proceeded down the side of the structure, shattering braces and posts as it went. On reaching the lower floor, the "electric fluid" divided, with one branch running along a door jam and passing into the ground below the doorstep and the other continuing down the south wall and creating quite a hole

The 1904 Cape Enrage Lighthouse overlooks the turbulent waters that give the Cape its name.

Travel Instructions: From Route 915 in Albert County, take Cape Enrage Road and drive 6.3 kilometres to the Cape Enrage Interpretive Centre (506-887-2273), which offers rappelling, climbing, zip-lining, and a restaurant. The cape is open year-round, and the services of the centre are available from mid-May through mid-October.

Established: 1840 (present tower 1904)

Position: 45.59392 N, -64.77992 W

Light: Green, on 1 s, eclipse 5 s

Tower Height: 9.2 metres

Focal Plane: 40.7 metres

Description: White square pyramidal tower, red lantern

upon entering the ground. Had the lightning struck a bit higher, it might have destroyed the lantern and lens, but as it was the damage was judged "comparatively trifling."

During an inspection in 1877, Agent Harding found that Keeper Starratt had hired a new man to serve as engineer in place of his son. Harding was not pleased with this action and let it be known that no keeper should hire an assistant without first notifying the department. Otherwise, the department would be "liable to have inefficient and incompetent, as well as unauthorized persons, placed in charge of valuable and important machinery and stations." Still, Agent Harding believed Starratt to be a reliable and efficient man and thought highly of his family. "He has a very intelligent and interesting family," Harding wrote, "and one could not but regret that owing to the isolated position of the Station they are denied the privileges of social and religious intercourse."

Keeper Starratt was dismissed in 1888 for being absent from the station and neglecting his duty. Years later, a debate was held in the Canadian Senate over whether Keeper Starratt had been replaced simply because of his political leanings.

John Kelly constructed a third lighthouse, the one that stands today, at Cape Enrage in 1904 at a cost of $916.88. When its light was first exhibited, a fourth-order lens was in use, and petroleum vapour was being burned under an incandescent mantle.

Lloyd Bennett became head keeper at Cape Enrage in 1923, and for several years was assisted by his brother Oscar. One evening Lloyd was returning from Saint John, when he crested a hill overlooking the cape and was alarmed to see the lighthouse was dark. He sped to the station, lit the light, and then started to search for his brother. In the fog alarm building he discovered a few drops of blood, but thought surely his brother would not leave the station for a minor injury. As he headed home with a flashlight, he learned it wasn't just a minor injury when he came across Oscar's severed finger.

Oscar showed up shortly thereafter, saying he had planned to be back earlier but the doctor had taken too long treating his wound. While Oscar was sliding the compressor belt onto the engine pulley, his finger had got caught between the two and was instantly cut off.

A new duplex was built at Cape Enrage in 1952 to house the families of the two Coast Guard keepers who ran the station. By the 1980s, only one keeper was assigned to Cape Enrage, and in 1988 the light was automated and the station de-staffed.

Dennison Tate, a physics teacher at a Moncton high school and son of a former lighthouse keeper on White Head Island, would often visit Cape Enrage to hike, canoe, and climb the cliffs. During one such trip in 1992, he discovered the duplex at Cape Enrage was to be torn down. Tate stewed over the planned demolition during the summer and came up with a six-page plan for a student-run outdoor adventure program that would generate enough money to restore and maintain the station. Grants from a federal student summer works program allowed Tate to hire six students during the summer of 1993 to paint the outside of the duplex,

install new shutters, and construct a stairway down to the beach.

Little progress was made in 1994, but late that summer the province of New Brunswick, with the encouragement of Albert County Heritage Trust, announced it would purchase the station. Tate's group was given permission to launch its adventure program the following summer, and it has been operating ever since. The duplex, known as the Cape House, serves as a dormitory for the staff and houses a restaurant for visitors. A stairway to the lighthouse was completed in 1997, and a gift shop, known as the Whistle House, was built in 1999.

Dennison and his wife, Ann, retired from the project in 2008, but under their direction a generation of students developed invaluable life skills at Cape Enrage. Today, visitors continue to be treated to the thrill of climbing, rappelling, and zip-lining in a spectacular setting perfectly suited for such activities.

65. Anderson Hollow

Anderson Hollow Lighthouse is the most well-travelled lighthouse in New Brunswick. Originally located on shore near a wharf in Waterside, the surviving lighthouse was preceded by two other towers that succumbed to the elements before this tower was built in 1903.

The *Annual Report of the Department of Marine* for 1889 provides the following information on the first Anderson Hollow Lighthouse that commenced operation that year with Reverend S. C. Moore as keeper:

> *A beacon light was…established at Anderson's Hollow, Chignecto Channel, in the County of Albert, and put in operation on the first day of August last. The light is fixed red, elevated 25 feet above high water mark, and visible a distance of 6 miles. The lighthouse tower is*

Anderson Hollow Lighthouse in its original location on the pier at Waterside. (Library and Archives Canada)

Travel Instructions: From Route 915 in Harvey turn northeast onto Mary's Point Road. Anderson Hollow Lighthouse will be visible on the left after 1.6 kilometres.

Established: 1889 (present tower 1903)

Position: 45.73518 N, -64.69728 W

Light: Inactive since 1909

Tower Height: 9.4 metres

Description: White square pyramidal tower, red lantern

Anderson Hollow Lighthouse at Harvey Bank Heritage Shipyard Park, its fourth and hopefully final home, 2011.

asquare wooden building, painted white, with red roof, and is 30 feet high from the wharf to the vane. The light is intended to guide vessels in the harbour of refuge behind the breakwater. Vessels may run for the harbour one hour before high water, giving the light 50 feet of a berth on the port hand.

In 1891, just two years after it was built, the lighthouse was damaged by a heavy storm, but it was repaired and strengthened at a cost of twenty-three dollars. Even with this strengthening, the tower was torn from its foundation the following year but again survived and was returned to its spot on the wharf. A new window was added to the tower in 1894 to increase the arc over which its light was visible, but all the repairs and improvements were for naught as a gale on November 21, 1895, carried away the end of the pier and the lighthouse.

A new tower, square in plan, with sloping sides and surmounted by a square wooden lantern, was erected on the repaired public wharf in 1898 to replace a temporary pole light that had been maintained since the former tower was lost. This lighthouse was destroyed by a storm on January 12, 1902, and a pole light was shown from the outer end of the breakwater until a new tower could be built.

After losing two towers, the marine department decided to place the third lighthouse on the shore north of the breakwater and directly opposite its outer end.

This lighthouse, constructed by W. C. Anderson of Waterside for $362, was a similar wooden, pyramidal tower and first exhibited its fixed white light at the opening of navigation in 1903.

A light to mark the outer end of the breakwater was apparently still deemed beneficial as in 1907 a seventh-order Chance anchor lantern, hoisted atop a 6.7-metre pole, went into operation. In 1909, the light shown from the 1903 tower was permanently discontinued, its function having been replaced by the mast on the breakwater.

The 1903 Anderson Hollow Lighthouse remained in its position on the bank until at least 1947, for the *List of Lights* for that year states: "if for any reason it becomes impossible to show this fixed white light from the end of the breakwater, a fixed red light will be shown temporarily from the lighthouse on shore."

At some point, the lighthouse was moved to the nearby property of Herbert Armstrong, where it stood next to the family's large Victorian house. Mr. Armstrong had served as keeper of Martin Head Lighthouse, where he and his wife raised five children.

Anderson Hollow Lighthouse next to the old Armstrong house, 1982. (Canadian Coast Guard)

The picturesque Anderson Hollow Lighthouse, 2008.

After the Victorian house was sold in the 1960s, the lighthouse quickly fell into disrepair.

By the 1980s, the lighthouse and adjacent home were owned by Marty and Elizabeth Tener, who recognized the historic value of the lighthouse and sought to donate it to the Albert County Heritage Trust. With the guidance of Mary Mijka, a grant was acquired to cover the cost of the move, and in 1987 the lighthouse was relocated to the intersection of Route 114 and Route 915 in Riverside-Albert.

Finally, on October 31, 2001 (a number of people thought it was a Halloween prank), the lighthouse was moved, most likely for the last time, to Harvey Bank Heritage Shipyard Park, on nearby Mary's Point where Shepody River meets Shepody Bay. The lighthouse was fixed up, an old wharf was reconstructed on the former shipbuilding site, and a replica of an old sailing ship was added along with attractive fencing and a picnic area, making this one of the most photogenic lighthouses in New Brunswick.

66. Grindstone Island

The upper portion of the Bay of Fundy between New Brunswick and Nova Scotia is known as Chignecto Bay. Towards its northern limits, this bay is forked, with the tip of the dividing peninsula known as Cape Maranguin. The entrance to the western fork, known as Shepody Bay, is defined by Cape Maranguin to the east and Grindstone Island to the west.

An 1847 report of the area noted:

The ledges of Sandstone at Cape Maranguin furnish Grindstones of superior quality, and the business of making them is prosecuted to some extent. A number of persons engaged in making Grindstones reside on the Cape, and each man makes on the average four hundred Stone, by measurement, during the season. … The Grindstones when made, are principally bought by persons from the opposite shore of Nova Scotia, at the South Joggins, and shipped to the United States, where they are in high repute and extensively used for grinding and polishing tools and cutlery.

The grindstone trade was also pursued on Grindstone Island and is how the island obtained its name.

A petition from sixteen inhabitants of Westmorland County calling for the establishment of a lighthouse on Cape Maranguin was presented to the New Brunswick government in 1847. A similar petition was submitted in 1849, and this was followed in 1854 by a petition of nineteen ship owners and shipmasters calling for a lighthouse on Grindstone Island. After additional petitions were received in 1885, £400 was finally allocated to erect a lighthouse on either Cape Maranguin or Grindstone Island.

Grindstone Island, which could also mark the entrance to Five Fathom Hole, the only safe harbour of refuge on the eastern side of the upper bay, was selected as the site. St. Ann's Church of Sackville owned the island and had leased it to Isaiah Bacon, who in turn had leased it to Dorchester Freestone Manufacturing. After a

Grindstone Island Lighthouse, 1911. (Library and Archives Canada)

half-acre of land was finally obtained, plans were drawn up in early 1859, and a contract for a lighthouse and keeper's dwelling was made with Jonathan R. Stevens.

The following Notice to Mariners was published in 1859 to announce the establishment of Grindstone Island Lighthouse:

Notice is hereby given, that on and after Thursday Night, the 20th October instant, a fixed White Light will be exhibited from sunset to sunrise in the Lantern on the Wooden octagonal Light Tower, sixty feet above the level of high water, lately erected on the western point of Grindstone Island in Chignecto Bay, in latitude 45 43' 13" N., longitude 64 37' 25" W. The octagonal Tower is painted white as is also the Keeper's House, one story, situated about 50 feet to the eastward of the Tower.

The first keeper of the light, which was produced by four lamps backed by twenty-two-inch reflectors, was James Clark, who served until 1873, when he resigned his position due to his wife's poor health.

In July 1876, John H. Harding, marine agent in Saint John, visited Grindstone Island to select a site for a steam fog alarm. J. B. Stevens constructed a coal shed and fog signal building the following year, and F. W.

Lantern being removed and relocated to the Coast Guard base in Saint John in 1994. (Canadian Coast Guard)

Grindstone Island is the only hexagonal concrete lighthouse in New Brunswick.

Holmes of London, England, supplied the trumpet and necessary machinery. When the trumpet commenced operation in late 1877, it was found that the boiler was inadequate, and the fog alarm was discontinued until an addition to the building was made and a larger boiler installed. A pond was excavated in the swamp adjoining the lighthouse property, and underground pipe was laid to convey the needed water to a storage tank near the fog alarm.

In 1892, the lighthouse was moved closer to the keeper's dwelling, and a new fog alarm building was constructed near the tower, on the extreme southwest point of the island. A modern oil diaphone plant replaced the steam fog alarm plant in 1916–1917.

A short article in the November 15, 1911, edition of the *Boston Daily Globe* reported that one of the four

lamps in use at Grindstone Island had exploded and set fire to the wooden lighthouse, driving the keeper and his assistant from their post. This loss necessitated the construction of the present Grindstone Island Lighthouse that sports a design unique to New Brunswick: a concrete hexagonal tower, with six buttresses. Work on this tower, atop which a fourth-order dioptric illuminating apparatus was installed, was carried out in 1911 and 1912 by day labour under W. F. Fitzgerald.

W. Wainright "Pappy" Weston became keeper in 1950, taking over from Hugh Wright. Keeper Wright's last entry in the logbook reads, "I am now packed up and ready to go after thirteen and a half years here as keeper, and I am not sorry to be leaving."

Keeper Weston and his wife, Ruby, raised five

children on Grindstone Island. Pappy was an accomplished fiddler, who was later inducted into the New Brunswick Country Music Hall of Fame, and his five children played musical instruments as well. Known as the Fundy Trailers, the six of them performed throughout New Brunswick.

The keepers had a radio transmitter on the island in 1952, and soon learned that people on shore could tune their personal radios and eavesdrop on the keepers' conversations with other stations. The keepers used this capability for their own benefit. When a keeper was ashore, he would monitor the station's radio transmissions and flash his house lights to answer questions: three times for yes, twice for no.

Sod was turned for two new dwellings and a fog alarm on July 1, 1959, and the Westons moved into their new home on November 18, 1959, the same day their old house was pushed over the bank and burned. A 7,500-watt generator arrived on the island on August 13, 1966, and just over a week later, the keepers' days of climbing the stairs in the tower every few hours were over. The Westons left Grindstone Island on March 31, 1970, just four months short of twenty years on the island. After boarding up the houses and engine room, Keeper Weston declared the station officially closed.

The lantern room was removed from the lighthouse in June 1984, shortly after the light was deactivated, and later placed atop a lighthouse constructed at the Saint

Travel Instructions: From Route 114 just west of Riverside-Albert, turn south on Route 915. After 3.5 kilometres, turn left onto Mary's Point Road and continue for 3.9 kilometres, passing Anderson Hollow Lighthouse, to reach Mary's Point Bird Sanctuary. A very distant view of Grindstone Island Lighthouse is possible near the interpretive centre, or you can follow a path down to the beach and hike out to the southeast part of Mary's Point at low tide for a closer view.

Established: 1859 (present tower 1912)

Position: 45.72178 N, -64.62102 W

Light: Inactive since 2001

Tower Height: 18 metres

Focal Plane: 28.3 metres

Description: White hexagonal tower with buttresses, red lantern

John Coast Guard base. Under pressure from local fishermen led by Keeper Weston, the tower was reactivated in 1986 sans lantern. On December 9, 1991, the current lantern, formerly used at Pease Island in Nova Scotia, was placed atop the tower. The reactivation of the light, however, was short-lived, as in 2001 the lighthouse was again extinguished.

67. Hopewell Wharf

Hopewell Wharf Lighthouse, 1922. (Library and Archives Canada)

Hopewell Cape is situated at the point where the Petitcodiac and Memramcook Rivers meet Shepody Bay. A wooden, pyramidal lighthouse, which stood four metres tall and displayed a fixed white light, was built on the public wharf at Hopewell Cape in 1915.

The tower was blown off the wharf in a gale on September 14, 1937, but its base was recreated and a new lantern placed on it in 1938. The *List of Lights* for 1954 shows the square tower still in use, but it was not listed in 1955.

68. Fort Folly Point

Fort Folly Point Lighthouse, 1934. (Canadian Coast Guard)

In 1888, bids were invited for constructing a lighthouse on Fort Folly Point, located at the southern tip of the peninsula that separates the Petitcodiac and Memramcook Rivers. E. C. Bowser of Dorchester built the lighthouse in 1889, and its first keeper, Andrea B. Richard, activated the light on March 1, 1890. The lighthouse consisted of a square, pyramidal tower, 10.7 metres tall, with an attached keeper's dwelling. The lighthouse was originally white with a red lantern, but a distinctive red horizontal band was later applied to the middle of the tower.

The original Fort Folly Lighthouse appeared in the *List of Lights* until 1964, after which a red skeletal tower was listed.

69. McFarlane Point

A wooden lighthouse was constructed at McFarlane Point on the eastern shore of the Petitcodiac River in 1909. The square tower had sloping sides and was surmounted by a square wooden lantern, from which a fixed white light was shown. Alexander McFarlane was its first keeper, and the light was active until being destroyed by fire on September 13, 1921. (An image for this lighthouse was not available.)

70. Outhouse Point

The Petitcodiac River derives its name from a Mi'kmaq word that means "the river that bends like a bow," and in 1909 a lighthouse was built on Outhouse Point, around which the river makes its most abrupt turn. Situated across the river from Moncton, Outhouse Point was named after one of the original settlers in the area.

Outhouse Point Lighthouse was a twin to McFarlane Point Lighthouse. The only major differences in the square, pyramidal towers were that Outhouse Point Lighthouse originally had a sixth-order lens, instead of a seventh-order lens, and it cost $738.90—$22.66 less than McFarlane Point Lighthouse.

Everett Taylor was responsible for the lighthouse during the Second World War. His two boys, Vaughn and Clarence, would often run the kilometre and a half out to the lighthouse after school, add a pint of kerosene to the lamp, light it, check for a clear light, and run back home. Keeper Taylor also served as an air raid warden, and when there was a perceived threat, the boys got to

Outhouse Point Lighthouse, destroyed by Coast Guard personnel in 1957. (Canadian Coast Guard)

skip their daily trek to the lighthouse.

No longer needed, Outhouse Point Lighthouse was toppled and set afire by the Coast Guard in 1957.

71. Pecks Point

Privately owned Pecks Point Lighthouse, 2011.

Pecks Point Lighthouse, 1908. (Library and Archives Canada)

Rockport Peninsula divides the northern extreme of the Bay of Fundy into two branches: Shepody Bay to the west and Cumberland Basin to the east. A lighthouse was proposed for the southern tip of the Rockport Peninsula, but instead one was built on Grindstone Island in 1859. This lighthouse marked Shepody Bay, but a light was still needed for Cumberland Basin.

In 1889, tenders were invited for a beacon light on Ward's Point, and the lighthouse, built by George Ingram, commenced operation at the opening of navigation in 1890 with Peter Hagen as its keeper. A small lens in the lantern room produced a fixed white light at a focal plane of 22.9 metres.

The department of marine decided the tower would better serve mariners if it were relocated from Wards Point, which was south of Rockport, to Pecks Point, just north of Rockport. This move occurred in 1908, and a diaphone fog alarm plant was installed in a building erected by Amos Lawrence of Sackville to supplement the light. E. R. Reid built a wooden dwelling for the fog alarm engineer in 1909.

The lighthouse is currently owned by Ken Tower, whose father relocated the tower and other station buildings over the winter ice from Pecks Point to their current location in 1958, after the light was discontinued in 1956. Ken has installed vinyl siding on the tower and keeps it and the entire property in immaculate condition. The keeper's house is on the adjacent property and belongs to his sister, while the station's old equipment shed sits between the two properties.

Travel Instructions: Pecks Point Lighthouse is located on private property near Rockport.

Established: 1890

Position: 45.75940 N, -64.48885 W

Light: Inactive since 1956

Tower Height: 6.7 metres

Description: White square pyramidal tower, red roof

72. Barnes Point
(Woody Point)

In 1911, John A. Lea was paid $983 to build a lighthouse on Barnes Point, which is situated along the eastern shore of Cumberland Basin, just south of Sackville. After the Coast Guard deactivated the light in 1976, the tower was sold and relocated to Nova Scotia, where it was greatly modified and incorporated into a summer residence near Amherst Shore.

Established: 1911

Position: 45.96441 N, -63.88144 W

Light: Inactive since 1976

Tower Height: 8.2 metres

Description: White square pyramidal tower, modified lantern room with red roof

Barnes (Woody) Point Lighthouse, 1934.
(Canadian Coast Guard)

Fort Monckton Lighthouse, circa 1930. (New Brunswick Museum, 1987.17.582)

NORTHUMBERLAND STRAIT AND GULF OF SAINT LAWRENCE

73. Fort Monckton

Fort Gaspareaux was built by French troops in 1751 to prevent the English from penetrating the Chignecto peninsula. In 1755, the fort fell to General Monckton's army, and was renamed in his honour. Rather than defend the outpost, the English burned it the following year.

In 1908, a lighthouse was built atop a square, cribwork foundation on the south side of the entrance to Gaspareaux River where the fort formerly stood. The National Historic Sites and Monuments Board erected a stone cairn near the lighthouse in the 1930s to commemorate the fort.

The top of the lighthouse caught fire one night in the late 1950s. Firefighters quickly doused the flames, but hours later the fire flared up again and consumed the tower. The present cylindrical tower commenced operation in 1972.

74. Indian Point Range Front 🚶
75. Indian Point Range Rear 🚗 🛑

Indian Point Range Front Lighthouse with a view of the red clay cliffs characteristic of the Northumberland Strait.

When the ferry terminal was completed at Cape Tormentine in 1917, the Cape Tormentine Entrance Range Lights were constructed just east of the ferry landing to work with the Cape Tormentine Wharf Range in guiding vessels to the terminal. The Cape Tormentine Entrance Range towers were square, pyramidal, wooden structures and had a vertical red stripe on their seaward face to indicate the range line.

Travel Instructions: From Highway 16, west of the Confederation Bridge take Exit 47 and drive east on Route 955 for 5.3 kilometres to Cape Tormentine Campground. Continue east on Route 960 for 2.5 kilometres to Vista Drive (unpaved) that leads to some cottages near the shore. The rear tower, surrounded by private property, is visible down an unpaved road just east of Vista Drive, while the front one is located down an unpaved road just west of Vista Drive.

Established: 1955

Position: Front: 46.10790 N, -63.77290 W; Rear: 46.10455 N, -63.77675 W

Light: Inactive since 1998

Tower Height: Front: 9 metres; Rear: 12.5 metres

Focal Plane: Front: 9.8 metres; Rear: 23.5 metres

Description: White square pyramidal towers, red lanterns

Deactivated several years ago, Indian Point Range Rear Lighthouse is starting to show signs of neglect.

In 1947, the Entrance Range lights were replaced by poles. Eight years later, towers similar to those used at the Entrance Range, were activated at Indian Point, just a few kilometres to the east. Each of the Indian Point towers had a red diamond painted on its seaward face as a daymark until 1966. Indian Point Range and the Entrance Range were discontinued in 1998.

76. Cape Tormentine Outer Wharf
77. Cape Tormentine Range Rear

The Cape Tormentine Outer Wharf Light is located on an abandoned ferry pier.

Cape Tormentine Rear Tower before being elevated in 1919. (Library and Archives Canada)

As part of the agreement that saw Prince Edward Island join Canada in 1873, the Dominion government agreed to provide year-round steamer service to the island. This was not problematic in the summer, but during the winter months, Northumberland Strait was often packed with ice. Small vessels known as iceboats, which were sheathed in metal and equipped with two rudder-like metal runners, were used to transport passengers and mail between Cape Tormentine and Cape Traverse starting in the winter of 1827. The iceboats were sailed or rowed across open water, and then pulled across the ice-covered sections by the crew and any male passengers who hadn't paid a premium fare.

In 1876, the steamer *Northern Light* started year-round service between Pictou, Nova Scotia, and Georgetown, Prince Edward Island, but during the winter, the vessel was often ice-bound. The New Brunswick & Prince Edward Island Railway reached Cape Tormentine in 1886, and working with the ice-boats, helped provide a reliable winter mail route to Prince Edward Island.

In 1897 the steamship *Stanley* began providing service between Cape Tormentine and Summerside, and range lights were established at Cape Tormentine in 1902 to guide the *Stanley* into port. The front light was shone from a window in the eastern gable of a freight shed on the railway pier, and the rear light was exhibited from a cupola atop the iceboat house, situated near the inner end of the pier.

Starting in 1906, the range lights were activated nightly, not just when needed by the *Stanley*. A lantern hoisted atop a mast became the front light that year, and in 1907, a new tower for the rear light was built 21.3 metres inland from the iceboat house. This square, wooden tower with sloping sides remains standing today.

In 1908, the front light was replaced by a 9.8-metre-tall tower equipped with a fourth-order lens. The upper portion of this pyramidal tower was wooden and painted white, while the lower portion was skeletal and painted red.

In 1917, ferry terminals were completed at Cape Tormentine and at Borden-Carleton on Prince Edward

The decommissioned Cape Tormentine Rear Range is one of the most endangered lighthouses in New Brunswick, 2008.

Travel Instructions: From Highway 16, west of the Confederation Bridge take Exit 47 and drive east on Route 955. After 4.8 kilometres, turn left near an old train depot onto Old Ferry Road. The rear tower will be on your right before the causeway that leads out to the Outer Wharf Lighthouse. The outer portion of the wharf is fenced to prohibit access.

Established: 1902

Position: Wharf: 46.13486 N, -63.77220 W; Rear: 46.13148 N, -63.78512 W

Light: Wharf: Red, on 1 s, off 1 s; Rear: Inactive since 1997

Tower Height: Wharf: 10.1 metres; Rear: 12.5 metres

Focal Plane: Wharf: 12 metres; Rear: 18 metres

Description: Wharf: White square tower, red lantern; Rear: White square pyramidal tower on timbers, red-roofed lantern

Island, and the railcar ferry *Prince Edward Island* began serving this route. The ferry was modified in 1922 to accommodate automobiles in addition to railcars.

The Cape Tormentine range lights were both raised in 1919. This is likely when the current woodwork was placed beneath the rear range light. The present front light, a short pepper-pot style tower, was put in place in the 1940s.

After the completion of the Confederation Bridge in 1997, the Cape Tormentine–Borden Ferry was discontinued, and with it, the Cape Tormentine Pier Range Lights. At the request of local fishermen, the front light, now known as the Cape Tormentine Outer Wharf Light, was reactivated in 1998. After years of neglect, the rear tower has greatly deteriorated.

78. Cape Jourimain

Cape Jourimain Lighthouse with outbuildings. (Library and Archives Canada)

One of nine octagonal wooden lighthouses in New Brunswick, the Cape Jourimain Lighthouse is arguably the most beautiful thanks to its ornate cornice work. Badly in need of restoration, this lighthouse sits dangerously close to the Northumberland Strait on the New Brunswick side of the Confederation Bridge, seen here in the background.

In 1868, John Page, chief engineer of public works, visited Northumberland Strait and examined Indian Point, Cape Tormentine, and Cape Jourimain to select a site for a lighthouse. Page recommended that a tower be built on Cape Jourimain, preferably of non-combustible materials, with a detached keeper's dwelling. The projected cost for the station was $8,500 for a stone tower and only $3,500 for a wooden tower.

The less expensive plan was selected, and the station was completed during 1869 except for the installation of the lighting apparatus, which failed to arrive that year. John Bent was appointed keeper, and on May 15, 1870, he started exhibiting a temporary light until three lamps set in twenty-three-inch reflectors were installed on June 7. A right-of-way to the lighthouse was purchased for two hundred dollars from M. Allen, and work on a road to the lighthouse commenced in 1872.

Early in the morning of June 14, 1875, Keeper Bent and three other men left Summerside on Prince Edward Island in the station's sailboat bound for Cape

Jourimain. About three kilometres out, the boat capsized, spilling its occupants into Northumberland Strait. A rowboat was sent out from Summerside, and after a hard pull, reached Bent's sailboat, which was on the bottom with its mast protruding from the water. No trace of the crew was evident near the boat, but Keeper Bent's body washed ashore later that day.

The station's boat was recovered, but the cost of repairs was such that a boat formerly used at Quaco Lighthouse was sent to Cape Jourimain. Silas Ross served as temporary keeper until Arthur W. Bent, son of John Bent, was hired.

The original lantern room, whose size prevented the keeper from easily trimming the lamps, was replaced with a larger one in 1876. The fixed white light was upgraded that same year to circular-wick lamps set in three twenty-four-inch reflectors and four twenty-two-inch reflectors. The seven lamps proved too many, as the excessive heat broke several glass panes in the lantern room, and the number was quickly reduced to five.

On June 15, 1878, the characteristic of the light was changed from fixed white to flashing white through the installation of a revolving apparatus equipped with four lamps and reflectors. Keeper Bent's salary was raised from $250 to $300 owing to the increased labour required by the new light.

In 1910, the lighthouse was moved to a new site to escape erosion. The illuminating apparatus was improved in 1914 through the installation of a fourth-order dioptric lens.

Cape Jourimain Lighthouse was automated in 1970 and then decommissioned in 1997 with the opening of the Confederation Bridge. The wooden, octagonal lighthouse was designated a federal heritage building in 1991 due, in part, to "classically inspired details such as the elongated bracketed cornice, the use of belt courses and crown trims and the prominent gallery guardrail."

Although the Cape Jourimain Nature Centre now surrounds the lighthouse, the Coast Guard remains responsible for the tower. Before applying for ownership of the tower, the centre hired a consulting firm in 2011 to determine the feasibility of restoring the historic tower and moving it back from the eroding shoreline.

Travel Instructions: From Highway 16, take the last exit before the Confederation Bridge to arrive at Cape Jourimain Nature Centre and Visitor Information Centre (506-538-2220). The 1.8-kilometre Lighthouse Trail loop leads to the lighthouse.

Established: 1870

Position: 46.15724 N, -63.80636 W

Light: Inactive since 1997

Tower Height: 13.7 metres

Focal Plane: 21.9 metres

Description: White octagonal tower, red lantern

79. Pointe-du-Chêne Range Front
80. Pointe-du-Chêne Range Rear

Front and Rear Pointe-du-Chêne Lighthouses. When mariners see one light above the other, they know they are in the proper channel.

Travel Instructions: Take Exit 37 from Route 15 and travel north on Route 140, which will become Parlee Beach Road, for 4.2 kilometres to the shore. From June through September, a fee is charged for parking at Parlee Beach.

Established: 1895 (current towers 1898)

Position: Front: 46.24072 N, -64.51169 W; Rear: 46.23941 N, -64.51199 W

Light: Fixed red

Tower Height: Front: 8.2 metres; Rear: 11.9 metres

Focal Plane: Front: 7.9 metres; Rear: 13.6 metres

Description: White square pyramidal towers with red vertical stripe on seaward face, red lanterns

Although Shediac is known today as "the Lobster Capital of the World," it has been home to many industries that exploited the protected waters of Shediac Bay. New Brunswick's first steam sawmill was built in 1820 on the Scoudouc River, which empties into Shediac Bay, and two decades later fifteen mills were operating near Shediac and exporting several million feet of lumber each year. Ferry service connected Prince Edward Island to Shediac between 1858 and 1917, and in 1937, Pan American Airlines began the first commercial flights between North America and Europe, using Shediac Bay as a refuelling stop for its flying "clipper" ships.

Pointe-du-Chêne Wharf opened in 1857 as the northern terminus of the European and North American Railway. Situated on the southeast side of the entrance to Shediac Bay, Pointe-du-Chêne was originally known as

Oak Point, but to distinguish it from the numerous other places bearing that name, its French spelling was adopted.

A pole light was mounted on Pointe-du-Chêne Wharf in 1860, and in 1875 range lights were erected to guide ships from Shediac Island Range to the wharf. Three thousand dollars had been appropriated for a lightship to mark this critical turning point, but it was found that range lights could serve the purpose at a great savings.

On August 29, 1895, range lights, in the form of lanterns hoisted atop masts, were established on the beach at Pointe-du-Chêne, about three kilometres east of Pointe-du-Chêne Wharf. To enter Shediac Harbour, vessels would steer for Cassie Point Lighthouse until they could bring the new Pointe-du-Chêne Range Lights into alignment. Mariners were then directed to follow these range lights until they reached the alignment of Shediac Island Range Lights, which would lead to Pointe-du-Chêne Wharf Range Lights. In 1898, the mast lights at Pointe-du-Chêne were replaced by a pair of square, pyramidal towers topped by square lanterns.

On October 1, 1899, a vessel hired from the Charlottetown Steam Navigation Company at a cost of five dollars per day was moored off Pointe-du-Chêne to serve as the Zephyr Rock Lightship. This schooner was painted blue with black bulwarks and displayed two white lights between its masts to warn vessels of dangerous Zephyr Rock. The lightship was used during the dark nights of late autumn between 1899 and 1903 "to facilitate the entrance to Shediac of the mail steamer from Prince Edward Island."

Of the three sets of historic range lights built to guide vessels into Shediac Harbour, only Pointe-du-Chêne Range Lights remain standing. A decorative lighthouse has been built on Pointe-du-Chêne Wharf as part of a modern set of range lights.

81. Shediac Island

On July 1, 1869, Henry Hendrickson first lit two minor lights on Shediac Island to mark the channel into Shediac's outer bay. Meier Robinson took charge of the lights in 1874 and served for nearly fifty years. An article in the *Daily Telegraph* noted that Keeper Robinson's twelve-year-old daughter drowned in 1885 while skating across the bay to school at Pointe-du-Chêne. She made a wrong turn and fell through a patch of thin ice. According to the account, "A little basket and the child's mitts were found in the hole [and] were the only evidence of the sad fate of little Annie Robinson."

Lightning destroyed one of the two mast lights on Shediac Island in 1892, forcing a temporary structure

A vintage postcard image of Shediac Island Lighthouse. (Michel Forand)

to be used until enclosed towers were built in 1895. The front tower measured 11.3 metres from base to vane, while the rear tower was 4.9 metres taller.

By 1954, the rear tower had been replaced by a skeletal tower. The range lights were discontinued in 1964.

The town of Shediac believes that this is their old wharf light; however, an elderly neighbour recalls that it was moved by horse and wagon from the Bouctouche area in the mid 1930s.

82. Shediac Wharf

In 1914, range lights were established on the government wharf at Shediac. The front light was just a pole light, but the rear light was exhibited from a square, pyramidal tower with a height of ten metres.

83. Caissie Point

Caissie Point Lighthouse, 2011. A local group is working to assume ownership of the lighthouse.

Travel Instructions: From Grand-Digue follow Route 530 for 4.3 kilometres and then bear right onto Chemin de la Côte. Drive 0.2 kilometres then make a right onto Chemin Jaillet. Drive to the end of the road and then turn left to the lighthouse.

Established: 1872

Position: 46.31983 N, -64.51264 W

Light: Yellow, on 2 s, eclipse 2 s, on 2 s, eclipse 6 s

Tower Height: 13.6 metres.

Focal Plane: 13.9 metres

Description: White square pyramidal tower, red lantern

In an 1871 report, John H. Harding, marine agent at Saint John, noted that a light on Caissie Point was of "first importance" to the "large and extensive trade of the Strait of Northumberland and the Port of Shediac the present terminus of the European and North American Railway, and also the Port of call and discharge of the different steamers plying in the Gulf."

Three sets of range lights would eventually be constructed to guide traffic in Shediac Bay, but vessels would first use the more powerful Caissie Point Lighthouse to locate the entrance to the protected harbour. Caissie Point Light commenced operation on August 30, 1872, exhibiting a flashing white light produced by two banks of lamps and reflectors.

Charles P. LeBlanc was appointed the first keeper and resided in a dwelling attached to the square, pyramidal tower. Keeper LeBlanc served at Caissie Point until 1901, a total of thirty-eight years, and was frequently praised in the annual inspection reports. Some of the references to him include: "willing to carry out any instructions or advice given him in connection with his duties," "faithfully attending to his duties, and obliging in every respect," and "very attentive, and keeps the building in good order." The station was supplied with a boat in 1878 and a manual foghorn in 1900.

84. Cocagne Range Front

In the seventeenth century, Nicolas Denys, an explorer in New France, left the following description of a harbour on the northeast coast of present-day New Brunswick:

> Having passed a little island, one is well under shelter, and finds water enough. The anchorage is in front of a large meadow which makes a cover of reasonable extent where one is placed in shelter. I have named this place the River of Cocagne, because I found so much with which to make good cheer during the eight days which bad weather obliged me to remain there. All my people were so surfeited with game and fish that they wished no more, whether Wild Geese, Ducks, Teal, Plover, Snipe large and small, Pigeons, Hares, Partridges, young Partridges, Salmon, Trout, Mackerel, Smelt, Oysters, and other kinds of good fish. All that I can tell you of it is this, that our dogs lay beside the meat and the fish, so much were they satiated with it.

Cockaigne is the French equivalent of the English utopia, signifying an ideal place. Denys also noted the abundant trees that covered the flat land, and it would be this lumber that helped the settlement of Cocagne thrive.

Travel Instructions: The front range light is located on the south side of the Cocagne River, alongside Route 134.

Established: 1907

Position: 46.33523 N, -64.61510 W

Light: Temporarily discontinued in 2008

Tower Height: 7.7 metres

Focal Plane: 7.8 metres

Description: Square, pyramidal tower, red lantern, red vertical stripe

Deactivated in 2008, Cocagne Range Lights may be reinstated if channel conditions change.

In 1907, the department of marine announced:

Range lights will be established at Cocagne. The front light is to be shown from an inclosed [sic] tower standing on the shore on the south side of the mouth of Cocagne river, 70 feet eastward of Cocagne bridge. The tower is a wooden building, square in plan, with sloping sides, surmounted by a square wooden lantern, the whole painted white…The back light stands on the shore of the river, 865 feet from the front light, and is shown from an anchor lens lantern hoisted on a pole. A diamond shaped beacon is attached to the pole to make it more conspicuous as a day mark.

The range lights were discontinued in 2008 due to shoaling of the channel.

85. Bouctouche (Buctouche) Bar

Original Bouctouche Bar Lighthouse. (Library and Archives Canada)

An eleven-kilometre hike along the beautiful Bouctouche Dunes brings you to this active lighthouse.

Lengthy Bouctouche Sandbar protects the waters of Bouctouche Bay. Its southern tip lies 1.5 kilometres off Saint-Thomas-de-Kent, near where the Point Dixon Range Lights were established in 1881 to help vessels locate the bay's entrance.

Several years later, the department of marine reported that a lighthouse had been built to mark the sandbar:

> A lighthouse on the southern extremity of Buctouche sand bar was put in operation on October 10, 1902. The lighthouse is a square wooden building, surmounted by a square wooden lantern rising from the middle of the cottage roof. The building and lantern are painted white. The lighthouse is 35 feet high from its base to the ventilator on the lantern, and is located on land 4 feet above high water mark. The light is fixed white dioptric, elevated 38 feet above high water mark, and visible 11 miles from all points of approach by water. The work was done by Mr. G.W. Palmer, of Kars, whose contract price for the building was $1,289.

In 1907, pilework was put in place to protect the lighthouse from the encroaching sea, and the boathouse was moved back to a safer position the following year. The present tower replaced the original Bouctouche Bar Lighthouse in 1959.

Travel Instructions: The lighthouse can be reached by a 22-kilometre roundtrip hike starting at Irving Eco-Centre: La dune de Bouctouche, or viewed at a distance from Saint-Thomas-de-Kent.

Established: 1902 (present tower 1959)

Position: 46.46115 N, -64.61243 W

Light: White, on 1s, eclipse 3 s

Tower Height: 11.4 metres

Focal Plane: 11.0 metres

Description: White square pyramidal tower, red-roofed lantern

86. Dixon Point Range Front
87. Dixon Point Range Rear

Rear tower before being relocated and restored, 2009.

Travel Instructions: Take Route 535 to the community of Saint-Thomas-de-Kent. The Dixon Point Lighthouse is located between civic addresses 4618 and 4624. The inactive rear tower is located a few houses to the north.

Established: 1881

Position: Front: 46.45692 N -64.65099 W; Rear: 46.45786 N, -64.65200 W

Light: Front: white, on 1s, eclipse 4 s; Rear: Inactive

Tower Height: Front: 8.3 metres; Rear: 10.4 metres

Focal Plane: Front: 10.4 metres; Rear: 12.5 metres

Description: White square pyramidal towers, red lanterns

François and Charlitte LeBlanc arrived in present-day Bouctouche on June 24, 1785, and carved a cross in a pine tree to mark the establishment of an Acadian village. The Mi'kmaq had previously named the area Chebooktoosk, meaning "great little harbour." A corrupted version of this name, Bouctouche, was applied to the bay and its major river, which have sustained the village through the years.

The construction of a pair of range lights to guide vessels into Bouctouche Harbour was noted in an 1881 department of marine report:

A contract was entered into with Mr. John Ward, builder, Shediac, for the construction of two wooden range light towers at Buctouche, and was satisfactorily executed by him, the contract price being $730. These lights stand on Dixon's Point, on the south side of Buctouche Harbour, and guide vessels into the Harbour. The front building is situated on the point near the old beacon, and consists of a square wooden tower 30 feet high. The light is fixed, white, catoptric, elevated 36 feet above high water mark, and should be visible 11 miles in the direction of the range.

The back range light is distant 1,050 feet northwest by north from the other, the building is similar and a light of the same description is shown, elevated 41 feet above high water, and visible 12 miles.

Dixon Point Range Lights replaced a set of day beacons and were first lit on June 9, 1881, by Keeper Thaddee B.

While the Dixon Point Range Lights were decommissioned in 1986, the front tower was later reactivated to assist vessels entering the Bouctouche Harbour.

Twenty-four years of neglect were taking their toll on the rear range, but in 2010 it was relocated and beautifully restored. It now sits along the shore of the bay a short distance from the former front range.

Robichaud. The range lights were discontinued in 1986, but the front tower was later reactivated as Dixon Point Light.

The rear tower was in poor condition when Andre and Yvette Maillet purchased it in 2005 for one dollar. Four years later, Joe Leger acquired the tower from the Maillets for one hundred dollars. Using a crane, the tower was placed on a flatbed truck and moved a short distance to Leger's seaside cottage, where it was set atop a concrete foundation. The inactive tower has been beautifully restored, inside and out, by the Legers.

88. Pointe à Jérôme Range Front 🚗
89. Pointe à Jérôme Range Rear 🚶 🛑

The freshly painted front and rear Pointe à Jérôme lights, 2009. The front tower is the only one of this design remaining in New Brunswick.

Travel Instructions: From Highway 11 in Bouctouche, take Exit 32 and travel east on Boulevard Irving. Once the road becomes Chemin Du Couvent (Route 475), follow it for 3.5 kilometres. The front tower is on the seaward side of the road and the rear tower in a field on the opposite side.

Established: 1883 (current rear tower 1916)

Position: Front: 46.48663N, -64.67882 W; Rear: 46.48910 N, -64.68233 W

Lights: Fixed white

Tower Height: Front: 6.3 metres; Rear: 14.3 metres

Focal Plane: Front: 5.8 metres; Rear: 17.7 metres

Description: White square pyramidal towers with red vertical stripes on seaward face, red lanterns

Range lights were established on Dixon Point in 1881 to guide vessels to the entrance of Bouctouche Bay, and two years later, a second set was constructed at Pointe à Jérôme, also known as Church Point or Indian Point, to direct mariners into the bay. An 1883 department of marine report describes the original Pointe à Jérôme Range Lights:

Two range lights were established during the past season upon Church or Indian Point, on the north side of Buctouche Harbour, on the Straits of Northumberland. Both lights are fixed white catoptric, and shown from small square wooden towers 23 feet high, the front light being visible in the line of range for 9 miles and the back

light for a distance of 12 miles. The lights are 660 yards apart and in range lead into the harbour through the deepest channel, clear of all obstructions, from the line of range of the Dixon Point Lights to the point where the channel turns abruptly to the westward to enter the Buctouche River.

Dosithee O. Maillet was appointed first keeper of the range lights at an annual salary of $150. Until 1916, both towers were listed as seven-metre-tall towers, but that year the range lights were moved to align with the axis of a new channel, and the rear tower was subsequently described as a skeletal steel tower with an enclosed watch room and slats on its seaward side.

90. Richibucto Head (Cap Lumière)

The 1865 tower and station. (Université de Moncton)

Richibucto Head Lighthouse, 2011.

In the early 1800s, Richibucto was the third-largest shipping port in New Brunswick. One shipbuilding family, the Jardines, built Richibucto's first square-rigged vessel, the *Ellen Douglas*, in 1819 and would launch over one hundred vessels before business declined in the 1880s.

In 1857, New Brunswick's House of Assembly authorized construction of a lighthouse on Richibucto Head at a cost of £250. Work on the project was delayed until May 1861, when John Wilkinson was dispatched to select a suitable place for the lighthouse. Wilkinson visited three sites and determined that a sandy point, six kilometres southeast of the entrance to Richibucto Harbour, was the most favourable position. This preferred site could be acquired at little cost as it was "deemed worthless for any other purpose," but the low-lying land would require a tall lighthouse, and it was not selected. Instead, the lighthouse was constructed on Richibucto Head, a short distance south of the point, where a shorter tower could be used and where the lighthouse could be maintained at less expense given the proximity to a settlement.

Amos Keith was awarded a contract of $592 to construct the lighthouse by July 1, 1863. The contract

Travel Instructions: From Highway 11 in Rexton, take Exit 53 and travel 1.5 kilometres north on Route 134 and then turn right onto Centennial Avenue. After 3 kilometres Centennial Avenue will bear right and become Route 505. Continue 11 kilometres to the shore and then turn left and drive 1.1 kilometres to the lighthouse.

Established: 1865 (present tower 1934)

Position: 46.66981 N, -64.71167 W

Light: White, on 0.5 s, eclipse 4.5 s

Tower Height: 10.5 metres

Focal Plane: 18.1 metres

Description: White square pyramidal tower, red lantern

specified that the tower "be of quadrangular form, strongly built of wood, anchored to a foundation of masonry measuring 16 feet on each side at the base. The height of the focal plane of the light above the ground will be 42 feet, and about 70 feet above the level of high water."

Amos Keith fulfilled his contract, but the lantern and lighting apparatus were not ready for shipment aboard a vessel bound from Britain to Richibucto in the spring of 1864, so the items were sent to Saint John instead. When the fourth-order lens arrived in Saint John, authorities considered installing it in that city's Harbour Beacon and transferring the reflectors in use there to Richibucto. This plan, however, was rejected, and the lens was shipped to Richibucto, where it first illuminated the night sky on May 2, 1865.

Fabian Richard served as the light's first keeper, and in 1875 it was noted that he had a family of eight, besides a married son and his son's wife, who also lived with them. Peter F. Richard became the second keeper of the lighthouse in 1895 and served until 1934, when the present tower was built.

91. Richibucto Beach

The entrance to the Richibucto River is bounded by two sandbars, and range lights were established on the southern one in June 1879. The front light consisted of a square wooden tower, ten metres tall, with an attached dwelling, and the rear light was displayed from an open-frame tower. In 1901, the original range lights were replaced with two new pairs of range lights as the channel had shifted and additional lights were needed to mark it. The range lights had to be relocated several times to track the ever-shifting channel.

Multiple sets of modern range lights were guiding mariners into the Richibucto River in 2011. (An image of the 1879 tower was not available.)

92. Pointe Sapin

Pointe Sapin Lighthouse and a modern metal tower work together to guide mariners into the local harbour.

Travel Instructions: From Highway 11, take Exit 74 and travel 32.2 kilometres on Route 117 to the lighthouse, located at the harbour.

Established: 1903 (present tower 1910)

Position: 46.96373 N, -64.83045 W

Light: Fixed yellow

Tower Height: 8.7 metres

Focal Plane: 11.3 metres

Description: White square pyramidal tower with red vertical stripe, red lantern

Pointe Sapin was originally known as Point-aux-Sapins, presumably due to the presence of fir (sapin) trees. Attracted by rich fisheries and fertile soil, settlers arrived in Pointe Sapin in 1860. The 1903 department of marine report records the establishment of a light at Pointe Sapin:

A pole light, established in the settlement of Sapin point, at the north extremity of Kouchibouguac bay, was put in operation on May 28, 1903, and will hereafter be maintained whenever fishing operations are being conducted in the neighbourhood.

The light is fixed white, shown from a seventh order lens lantern hoisted on a pole. It is elevated 50 feet above high water mark and should be visible 12 miles from all points of approach by water.

The pole...stands 50 feet back from the edge of the sandstone cliff which forms the shore; between Messrs. Loggie's lobster factory and the Roman Catholic church.

Fishermen were notified that they could run for the light between the bearings of 248° and 338°. Remaining within this 90° arc would keep them clear of the southern end of Sapin Ledge and a reef south of the light.

In 1910, an 8.2-metre-tall, square tower, built under contract by James Legoof for $440, replaced the pole light. This new light was also fixed white but produced by a sixth-order lens. In 1941, a front light was added to range with the tower and indicate the proper approach to the harbour.

93. Point Escuminac

Point Escuminac marks the southern entrance to Miramichi Bay, and, along with North Point on Prince Edward Island, defines the northern entrance to Northumberland Strait. The name Escuminac is derived from a Mi'kmaq word meaning "watching place" or "look-out place."

During an address in 1820, George S. Smyth, Lieutenant-Governor of New Brunswick, informed the House of Assembly that he would take the requisite steps to see a lighthouse built on Point Escuminac. Twenty years later the lighthouse had not been built, likely because no law had been passed for levying duties on shipping at Miramichi to pay for its maintenance. New Brunswick had been collecting lighthouse duties at ports on the Bay of Fundy for years, and these funds had paid for the maintenance and construction of nine lighthouses by 1840.

A petition for a lighthouse on Point Escuminac was brought before the House of Assembly in 1840 signed by the two most prominent merchants of the Miramichi area, Gilmour Rankin and Joseph Cunard, and one hundred other citizens. This spurred the House to grant £600 for the project, and work commenced on the point later that year. In 1841, another £748 was allocated for the lighthouse, and it finally commenced operation on August 12 of that year, the tenth lighthouse in the colony and first on its northern coast. The total cost of the lighthouse and keeper's dwelling came to £1,795, which included a supply of oil and six months' salary for the keeper. Thus another £447 had to be deducted from the lighthouse fund in 1842, but over £450 had been collected at ports on the Gulf of Saint Lawrence that year, which covered the cost.

The original Point Escuminac Lighthouse was an octagonal tower, made of hand-hewn lumber held together with wooden pins and covered with pine shingles. Six Argand lamps and reflectors were employed

Original Point Escuminac Lighthouse. (Library and Archives Canada)

in the lantern room to produce a fixed white light at a height of 21.3 metres above high water, and John McEwan was hired as the first keeper at an annual salary of £95. The lighthouse was quite isolated until £100 was provided in 1846 to complete a road to the station.

Point Escuminac Lighthouse was originally located 27.4 metres from the extremity of the point, which is composed of fragile sandstone. Prior to 1860, roughly a half metre of shoreline was lost to erosion each year, but during a great storm that year, nine metres were lost in a few hours, leaving just nine metres between the sea and the lighthouse. Fortunately, the sandstone shingles and boulders washed up by the storm built a thick wall around the station, but an even stronger storm in 1862 pushed this defensive work back to the lighthouse. The storm surge rose to the level of the ground floor of the dwelling and lighthouse, and Keeper William Hay felt his family was in imminent peril.

The relocation of the station to an elevated spot 122 metres inland was recommended and strongly backed by Keeper Hay, but the buildings remained right where they had been built until 1879.

Point Escuminac Lighthouse, 2011. This "apple-core" tower is the only one of its type in New Brunswick, although the design was also deployed at Cape Forchu in Nova Scotia and at Brighton Beach on Prince Edward Island.

In 1869, the original lantern and lighting apparatus, reported to be worn out and leaky, were replaced with a third-order French Fresnel lens and a new lantern at a cost of $1,301. A temporary light was exhibited while the change was effected.

A fog whistle went into operation at Point Escuminac on June 1, 1874. The whistle sounded ten seconds each minute during fog and was tended by Thomas Philips, who received an annual salary of eight hundred dollars for overseeing the light and fog alarm. The original keeper's dwelling was too small to accommodate Keeper Philips's family of eight, so an addition was built in 1875.

James Carter was placed in charge of the light and fog alarm in 1888. By this time, there was a meteorological station and signal station at Point Escuminac, which H. W. Phillips was paid $134 each year to operate.

Carter and Phillips were both dismissed in 1892 after charges were brought against them and confirmed during an investigation. Keeper Carter had submitted several fraudulent accounts to the department of marine, and Phillips had taken unauthorized leaves.

In a reply to his dismissal letter, Phillips congratulated the department in "getting rid of a great rascal in the person of the late keeper who has ignored the Departmental regulations since he came here and who

left his station in December last and did not return until the 5th inst. (April). And who no doubt got his full pay for leaving the valuable property at the mercy of the world." Phillips acknowledged his temporary absences but asked the department to reconsider. "I think that after my long service at this place being here for eighteen years in connection with this station the department might have pardoned me and tempered justice with mercy especially as the remuneration was so small for the work performed."

Kenneth R. McLennan took charge of all operations at Point Escuminac, including the signalling and meteorological stations, in 1892 for an annual salary of just $700, saving the department over $134 each year.

Around 2 A.M. on September 30, 1901, Captain John McCarthy of the schooner *Levinia* was making his way to Miramichi in a thick fog. When about a kilometre south of Point Escuminac, Captain McCarthy picked up the light but claimed the foghorn was not in opera-tion and did not sound until thirty minutes later when he passed north of the light. Upon reaching Newcastle, Captain McCarthy filed a complaint, which prompted an investigation by the department of marine.

Inspector John Kelly was dispatched to look into the matter. Six Miramichi Bay pilots testified that the foghorn, situated on the north side of the point, was often not audible south of the station, especially with an onshore breeze. However, the evidence that carried the most weight in exonerating Keeper McLennan was his own logbook, which showed that the fog alarm had been in operation from 11:10 P.M. on September 29th until 7:50 the following morning.

In 1906–1907, the fog alarm building was converted into an engine room for a new three-inch diaphone fog alarm plant, and an extension was added to house two fifty-horse-power boilers and a coal room. By 1935, the boilers were worn out, and an acetylene gun was used as a fog alarm for roughly five years, until a new air horn, powered by an oil engine, was installed.

Edward Rourke built a new keeper's dwelling and boathouse under contract in 1910 for $1,975, while T. Contour of Escuminac sank a well for $60. An electric lighting plant was installed in 1914.

A powerful light and a working foghorn couldn't prevent the terrible maritime tragedy known as the Escuminac Disaster. On the evening of June 19, 1959, fifty-four boats set out from Escuminac Harbour in pursuit of salmon. The 5 P.M. weather forecast did not anticipate the strength of the approaching storm, a hurricane that had remained offshore after passing over Florida until it strangely looped into the Gulf of Saint Lawrence. By the time a storm warning was issued, it was too late for the radio-less fleet, which had set their nets to drift for the night.

According to a news report, "The storm struck with sudden severity and the calm sea soon became a boil-ing cauldron of mountainous…50 and 60-foot waves, which tossed the small boats about like matchwood." Twenty-two fishing boats sank, and thirty-five men and boys drowned, leaving behind twenty-six widows and eighty-three fatherless children, a devastating blow to the small communities on the bay. A monument, inscribed with the names of the victims, stands near Escuminac Harbour today.

In early 1965, the Miramichi Historical Society learned of plans to demolish Point Escuminac Lighthouse and promptly wrote their Member of Parliament to see if they could acquire "the lantern, which consists of a series of prisms, etc., and which was made in Paris." The department of transport responded that the lens was to be installed at another station, but the society could have the lantern room. Unfortunately, the society was only interested in the lens, and thus no remnant of the origi-nal Point Escuminac Lighthouse, which was demolished in November 1966, remains in the area.

The present concrete, hexagonal lighthouse was built in 1966 and is the only example of this "apple-core" design in New Brunswick. The lighthouse was de-staffed in 1989.

94. South Tracadie

In 1876, Vital Arseneaux built two towers to guide vessels through South Tracadie Gully. These range lights commenced operation at the opening of navigation in 1877, with the front light being fixed white and the rear light fixed red. The front tower was an open-frame structure, standing 6.1 metres tall, while the rear tower was an enclosed, square tower with a height of 7.9 metres. The towers were painted to match the colour of the lights they displayed.

In 1896, the channel shifted ninety-one metres to the south, and the range lights, located on the north side of the gully, could not be positioned to indicate the channel so the front light was discontinued, leaving the rear light to serve as a coastal light. A lens was installed in the rear tower in 1911 in place of the reflectors formerly used, and by 1916 the red tower had received a

South Tracadie Lighthouse, 1920. (Library and Archives Canada)

horizontal white band. The tower last appeared in the *List of Lights* in 1958.

95. North Tracadie

At the turn of the nineteenth century, Tracadie Village, situated at the entrance to North Tracadie River, had a population of roughly two thousand and a substantial wharf that provided shipping facilities for the district. North Tracadie River and nearby South Tracadie River both feed into expansive but shallow lagoons that connect with the sea through narrow channels known as gullies.

In 1872, a square wooden tower was built at North Tracadie Gully, and William Archer lit its lamps for the first time in October of that year. James Mitchell, the inspector of lights for New Brunswick, visited the station in 1874, and recorded the following comment on the usefulness of the light and similar lights nearby: "During the short time they have been in operation, their friendly light has guided many a hardy fisherman in safety through the narrow gullies, and many lives and

North Tracadie Lighthouse, 1920. (Library and Archives Canada)

much valuable property—valuable, because it consists of their all—is yearly saved to these men by these lighthouses." On Mitchell's recommendation, a second light, displayed from an open-frame tower located seaward of the lighthouse, was established in 1875 to form a range to indicate the entrance to North Tracadie Lagoon.

The ever-shifting channel at North Tracadie Gully caused the department of marine much trouble. In 1893, the lights, which by this time consisted of an enclosed tower with a height of ten metres for the rear light and a lantern on a mast as the front light, were relocated to the south side of the gully. The following year, it was necessary to establish range lights, consisting of lamps hoisted atop poles, on the north side of the gully, while the enclosed tower was left on the south side to serve as a coast light.

In 1895, the range lights on the north side of the gully were discontinued, and the front light was returned to the south side of the gully to range with the enclosed tower. Incredibly, the channel shifted once again, and the tower and pole light were relocated to the north side of the gully in 1896.

In 1908, a fourth-order lens was installed in the tower in place of four lamps and reflectors. A pole light had replaced the tower by 1947.

96. Pokemouche

Pokemouche Village is situated on the Pokemouche River, roughly three kilometres from where the river enters the Gulf of Saint Lawrence through Pokemouche Gully. During 1875, a lighthouse, consisting of a square, 11.3-metre tower with an attached keeper's dwelling, was built on Pokemouche Island, just north of the gully, to guide mariners through the opening. Due to the lateness of the season, its keeper, Philip Robichau, did not activate the tower's fixed green light until the opening of navigation in 1876.

In 1884, a second light was established to work with the main light in indicating the proper alignment for entering the gully. The new light was a lantern, displaying a red light, which was hoisted atop a pole capable of sliding along a tramway so it could be moved to suit changes in the channel.

On April 27, 1939, Keeper Ferguson started a grass fire on the island that got out of control and burned down the lighthouse. An unwatched automatic light, shown from a lens lantern atop a pole, commenced operation a few weeks later. (An image for this lighthouse was not available.)

97. Portage Island

Two barrier islands bracket the main entrance to Inner Miramichi Bay: Portage Island to the north and Fox Island to the south. A square lighthouse on the southern end of Portage Island commenced operation on October 6, 1869, to mark this important passage.

A new lantern room and lens had recently been installed at nearby Point Escuminac Lighthouse, and its old lantern room was used to construct the lantern room for Portage Island Lighthouse. Four lamps with silvered parabolic reflectors, also from Point Escuminac, were employed at Portage Island.

No dwelling was provided for George Davidson, the first keeper. His only shelter on Portage Island was a small shed, which officials conceded was "not sufficient" in cold

Portage Island Lighthouse, 1920. (Library and Archives Canada)

On the grounds of the New Brunswick Aquarium and Marine Centre, Portage Island Lighthouse is visited annually by many schoolchildren.

weather. The original buildings on Portage Island cost $604.40, and an additional $300 was requested to build a small house for the keeper.

The dwelling was finally completed in May 1872, but it was destroyed by fire in February 1875. Keeper Davidson was dismissed the following August and replaced by Hugh Murray. While visiting the station later that year, the inspector noted, "the light here is not so well kept as formerly, as the present keeper does not understand keeping his lamps in proper order, but will likely improve in time." The lighthouse was also not as clean as usual, but this was attributed to workmen, who were using the lighthouse as a "sleeping apartment" while building the new keeper's dwelling.

During a visit in 1876, the inspector observed that the lighthouse and keeper's dwelling were still not receiving the necessary attention. The tidiness of the station differed very much from similar stations, "owing no doubt," the inspector concluded, "to the want of female assistance." This issue was soon addressed as the report the following year noted the keeper had "two female assistants, and everything looks neat and clean." In 1908, a mast light was placed on Portage Island to serve as a front range light when aligned with the existing lighthouse.

A modern tower was placed on Portage Island in the 1980s, and in 1986 the New Brunswick Aquarium and Marine Centre purchased the old lighthouse. Donald Boudreau of the Village Historique Acadien led the effort to disassemble the lighthouse into three pieces, transport it by boat to Burnt Church, and finally reconstruct the tower on a wharf near the aquarium in Shippagan.

Travel Instructions: From Route 113 in Shippagan, turn north onto Rue 12 and after one block turn left onto Avenue De l'Eglise and then make a right onto Rue De l'Aquarium, which terminates near the lighthouse.

Established: 1869

Position: 47.74802 N, -64.70904 W

Light: Inactive

Tower Height: 12.8 metres

Description: White square pyramidal tower, red lantern

98. Big Shippegan

The Big Shippegan Lighthouse, 2009.

The new 1905 tower with the old tower in the background. (Provincial Archives of New Brunswick)

In 1871, John Harding, agent of the department of marine at Saint John, urged the establishment of a light to mark a channel leading to Shippagan Harbour.

The importance of this channel to the large class of hardy fishermen who follow this branch of industry and use that channel so largely in going to and from the fishing grounds, can scarcely be overrated. As the water is not deep, great care must be employed in making the harbor, especially in a storm, even during daylight.

Some years ago I was called upon as the Coroner of that district to hold an inquest on the bodies of three brothers, who in attempting to enter this Gully in a Southern storm, from the want of a proper land mark to guide them safely into the harbor, touched on one side of the channel, and their boat was upset. The three found a watery grave. A Lighthouse erected on the inside island would be a guide by day as well as by night, and would without doubt, stimulate the trade of that important district, while furnishing at the same time a means of protecting life.

The following year a square wooden tower, six metres tall and topped by a wooden lantern, was constructed and equipped with four flat-wick lamps and reflectors to guide fishermen through Big Shippagan Gully. Keeper Francis Dumaresque exhibited the light for the first time on October 21, 1872.

During an inspection in 1875, Keeper Dumaresque, who had been described as "a very obliging and efficient officer," was absent from the station, having left the light in charge of another man so he could tend his crops. The lighthouse was not in as good a condition as it had been in previous years, and a letter was sent to the keeper chiding him for his neglect and advising him to personally supervise the light. Keeper Dumaresque was again absent from the station during the inspection visit of 1876, having left to visit his sick wife. The lighthouse was "found in very bad order, the plaster in the building broken very much, and the building generally very untidy." Keeper Dumaresque was at the station for the 1877 inspection, and everything was "neat and in good order," a condition at least partly attributed to the recovery of his wife.

A breakwater was built in 1875 to prevent the sea from undermining the lighthouse. This proved effective until a heavy storm in 1879 damaged the tower's foundation. The following year, Michael Hayden moved the lighthouse from an island called L'Islet to Alexander Point, on the northeast side of the gully. A lantern hoisted on a pole was placed 148 metres east of the relocated tower to form range lights to indicate the proper course through the gully.

A keeper's dwelling was built in 1883 and occupied by Keeper Dumaresque until his thirty-one years of service ended in 1902. The front light that operated in conjunction with Big Shippegan Lighthouse was discontinued in 1888, and the following year range lights were established on the south side of the gully.

In 1905, a much taller lighthouse was constructed ninety-one metres south of the old tower by Honore Duguay under a $1,500 contract. The new Big Shippegan Lighthouse, an octagonal tower, measured 15.5 metres from its base to the top of the ventilator on its red octagonal lantern and was situated on a square wooden cribwork. The lighthouse commenced operation at the opening of navigation in 1906, and the following year it was altered to receive a single-flashing third-order lens instead of its fourth-order lens.

Travel Instructions: From Shippagan continue north on Route 113 across the causeway to Lamèque Island, then take the first right onto Chemin Chiasson. After 4.6 kilometres, turn right onto Allee Domitein. After 0.8 kilometres, park and walk about a kilometre to reach the lighthouse.

Established: 1872 (present tower 1905)

Position: 47.72214 N, -64.66061 W

Light: Yellow, on 0.2 s, eclipse 4.8 s

Tower Height: 16.1 metres

Focal Plane: 15.6 metres

Description: White octagonal tower, red lantern

Big Shippegan Lighthouse is one of nine octagonal wooden towers remaining in New Brunswick. Although the tower's Fresnel lens is long gone, it still supports a beautiful Barbier, Benard, and Turenne lantern room.

99. Miscou Island

In 1853, the commissioners of lights for the Gulf of Saint Lawrence called for a lighthouse on Birch Point, the northeast point of Miscou Island. The lighthouse committee acknowledged the need for the light but regretted that the Lighthouse Fund did not permit the necessary outlay. Still, the committee recommended that the commissioners select a suitable site and submit an estimate for the work.

A petition from numerous merchants and inhabitants of Bathurst calling for a lighthouse on Miscou Island was presented to the House of Assembly in 1854. Joining this petition was a letter from the agent at Bathurst for Lloyd's, the noted marine insurer, which read in part,

> In view of the great number of casualties to shipping on the Island of Miscou, at the entrance of this Bay, and the consequent vast loss of property, it becomes a matter of some importance to endeavor to get a Light House established there as a means of averting these evils.

The commissioners for the Gulf of Saint Lawrence reported in 1854 that they had selected a site for the lighthouse and estimated the structure would cost £2,000. The lighthouse committee felt the only way to justify the outlay would be to raise the lighthouse tax by one penny to two pence per ton. With this increase in place, £1,200 was appropriated on March 31, 1855.

Construction of the lighthouse, keeper's dwelling, and a woodshed was opened to bids, and a £1,220 contract, stipulating that the work be done by September 1, 1856, was awarded to James Murray on August 25, 1855.

After the lantern arrived from England on October 10, 1856, Keeper William Hay from Point Escuminac Lighthouse was sent to Miscou Island to oversee the installation of eight lamps and reflectors. Keeper Hay placed the light into operation on November 4, and then passed responsibility for its care to George

Miscou Island Lightstation. The tower is seen here with its original lantern that was replaced in 1908. (Library and Archives Canada)

McConnell, who had been selected form a pool of thirteen applicants. The total cost for the wooden, octagonal lighthouse, which stood 22.6 metres tall, was £2,200.

During 1874, a wooden building was erected east of the lighthouse to house a steam fog whistle. The fog alarm commenced operation in June of 1875 issuing five-second blasts every thirty seconds when needed.

After more than twenty years of service at Miscou Island, Keeper McConnell passed away in 1877. Robert Rivers was then hired and given an annual salary of eight hundred dollars, from which he paid David Bell to run the fog alarm. Throughout 1888 the fog alarm was silent, owing to the need for a new boiler. When a larger boiler arrived the following year, significant alterations were needed to accommodate it, and the fog alarm did not resume operation until September 24, 1889.

A new catoptric illuminating apparatus, which revolved once every seventy-five seconds to produce four bright flashes spaced by fifteen seconds and followed by thirty seconds of darkness, was installed at Miscou

The tower at the Miscou Island Lighthouse is one of just two in New Brunswick that can be climbed by the public.

Travel Instructions: Follow Route 113 to its terminus at Miscou Island Lighthouse. The lighthouse is open from May through the long weekend in October.

Established: 1856

Position: 48.00936 N, -64.49297 W

Light: White, on 4 s, off 1 s

Tower Height: 25.3 metres

Focal Plane: 24.5 metres

Description: White octagonal tower, red lantern

Island in time for the opening of navigation in the spring of 1894. In 1908, the lighthouse tower was altered to accommodate a new lantern and Fresnel lens, manufactured in 1907 by Barbier, Benard, and Turenne of Paris, France. The third-order lens produced two flashes every 7.5 seconds in this manner: flash 0.5 second, eclipse one second; flash 0.5 second, eclipse 5.5 seconds.

The tower was moved sixty-one metres inland in 1946 to save it from erosion. In 2001, the lighthouse was closed to the public due to mercury contamination in the lantern room and lead paint in the soil surrounding the tower. The tower's Fresnel lens originally floated in a mercury bath, which allowed the lens to revolve with minimal effort. Part of the keeper's responsibilities was to filter the mercury, which resulted in small amounts of it being spilled on the lantern room floor.

The cleanup was scheduled to take a few days, but the lighthouse remained closed to the public for years. During the closure, the province of New Brunswick invested nearly two million dollars to make Miscou Island an eco-tourism destination. As part of this effort, the lighthouse received new interior stairs, a paved parking area, and washroom facilities. Miscou Island Lighthouse, with its inactive Fresnel lens still in place, was officially reopened just in time to host the opening ceremonies for the World Acadian Congress in August 2009.

MIRAMICHI BAY AND RIVER

100. Preston Beach

Preston Beach Front Tower, 1920. (Library and Archives Canada)

Range lights were established on the southern side of Miramichi Bay, roughly eight kilometres west of Point Escuminac, on September 30, 1869. The front light was displayed from a mast, while the rear light was exhibited from a barn. A black band painted on the barn's roof, when aligned with the front structure, provided a daymark for crossing the bar.

In 1898, the front light was placed atop a square, pyramidal tower, and a skeletal steel tower with an enclosed upper portion was constructed for the rear light. Modern skeletal towers were serving Preston Beach in 2011.

Preston Beach Rear Tower, 1920. (Library and Archives Canada)

101. Fox Island Ranges

Swashway range tower. (Canadian Coast Guard)

Two separate light stations once stood on Fox Island at the entrance to Miramichi Bay. In 1862, a pair of beacon lights was established near the northwest tip of Fox Island along with a keeper's dwelling. A second set of lights was placed on the eastern end of the island in 1872. To distinguish between them, the original lights were called Upper Fox Island, and the newer lights Lower Fox Island or Swashway, as they could be used to enter the Swashway Channel.

In 1881, a third light was added to Upper Fox Island, and mariners were instructed that lights Nos. 1 and 2 in line led to Horseshoe Channel, lights Nos. 1 and 3 in line led through Portage Island Channel, and lights Nos. 2 and 3 in line led to a buoy on Horseshoe Shoal. All five lights on Fox Island were originally lamps exhibited from masts, but in 1891 two square, skeletal towers with horizontal slatwork on their seaward face replaced the lights at Lower Fox Island.

In 1918, a wooden, square, pyramidal tower topped by a square lantern replaced one of the skeletal towers on Lower Fox Island. A skeletal, steel tower, surmounted by an enclosed watchroom and an octagonal wooden lantern, and with a square wooden lantern displaying a second light midway up the tower, started to serve as

1918 Upper Fox Island Tower, also known now as Portage Island Channel Range Rear Lighthouse.

Upper Fox Island light No. 3 that same year. Two pairs of range lights, including the 1918 Upper Fox Island tower, were active on Fox Island in 2011.

Travel Instructions: The lights on Fox Island are best seen by boat.

Established: 1862 (present tower 1918)

Position: 47.12848 N, -65.04204 W

Light: Fixed white

Tower Height: 19.9 metres

Focal Plane: 19.1 metres

Description: Skeletal-tower, enclosed upper portion

102. Newcastle (Lime Kiln Bank)

On July 1, 1884, a fixed red light, displayed from a square, wooden tower with a height of seven metres, commenced operation on the north side of the Miramichi River, just below Newcastle. The tower reportedly burned down in the 1940s. (An image for this lighthouse was not available.)

103. Oak Point Range Front

On May 17, 1869, two sets of range lights were established to guide vessels through Miramichi Bay and up the Miramichi River. The outermost set was placed at Oak Point, with Thomas Coughlan as their keeper, while the inner set was located at Grants Beach. The *Annual Report of the Department of Marine* noted, "The masters of the two lines of steam ships running up the Miramichi, speak highly of the advantage derived from them, in enabling them to navigate the river on the darkest night."

In 1904, R. A. Russell built enclosed towers at Oak Point to replace the lanterns shown from masts. These new lighthouses, square in plan with sloping sides and surmounted by square wooden lanterns, were placed in operation on October 6. The front tower was ten metres from its base to the top of the ventilator on its lantern and displayed its light at a focal plane of 13.7 metres above high-water mark. The rear tower, situated 549 metres from the front tower, stood 16.2 metres tall and had a focal plane of 18.3 metres.

Inactive since around 1953, the Oak Point Front Range Lighthouse has been moved seventeen kilometres west. An oversized cupola has replaced the tower's original lantern room, and an addition has been made to one side of the tower. Modern range lights stood on Oak Point in 2011. What became of the wooden rear tower is unknown at this time.

The altered Oak Point Range Front Lighthouse is privately owned but easily visible from the side of the road.

Travel Instructions: Take Route 11 to the northern side of the Miramichi River and continue east for 2.2 kilometres. The lighthouse is on private property but can be viewed from the side of the road without trespassing.

Established: 1869 (present tower 1904)

Position: 47.05074 N, -65.46835 W

Light: Inactive since 1953

Tower Height: 10 metres

Description: White square pyramidal tower, red lantern

104. Grant Beach Range Front
105. Grant Beach Range Rear

Grant Beach Rear Tower at its current location after renovations. (Gordon Burns)

Privately owned Grant Beach Front Tower, 2011.

The Miramichi River is the second-longest river in New Brunswick, and Miramichi, consisting of the amalgamated towns of Newcastle, Chatham, and several smaller communities, is the largest city in northern New Brunswick.

Much of the history of the area centres on Beaubears Island, located where the Miramichi River divides into its northwest and southwest branches. The island was a meeting place for the Mi'kmaq, a tragic Acadian refugee camp, a thriving shipbuilding centre, and is now a national historic site.

In 1765, William Davidson and John Cort arrived in the area from Scotland and established a fishery and shipbuilding business on Beaubears Island. Davidson won a lucrative contract to supply ship masts to the British Navy, and in 1773 launched the area's first ship, the *Miramichi*. The island would pass through several hands over the years, but shipbuilding remained its primary use, with John Russell building twenty-six ships on the island between 1837 and 1850.

Range lights were established at Grant Beach and Oak Point on May 17, 1869, to serve maritime traffic accessing the Miramichi River. Francis Russell was

hired as the first keeper of Grant Beach Range Lights at an annual salary of one hundred dollars.

Alexander Fitzgerald of Newcastle constructed enclosed towers at Grant Beach in 1903 to replace the lanterns shown from masts. A dioptric, seventh-order lens was used in the front tower, while a catoptric light was employed in the rear tower. When in range, the fixed white lights marked the channel from a conical buoy at the narrows of Sheldrake channel up to Malcolm Point.

Byron Savage, a veteran of the Second World War, became keeper of the range lights in 1961 upon the recommendation of the previous keeper, William Hay, who relocated to Ontario. Keeper Savage recalls his daily routine, for which he was initially paid an annual salary of $150. "Each evening I went to the top of each lighthouse, removed the glass globes and cleaned them. I would fill up the lamps with kerosene oil and then light the wicks with a match. I would place the lamps inside the lanterns, replace the globes and the lights were all set for the night. I would go back in the morning to put out the lights."

The wooden Grant Beach towers were replaced by modern structures in 1984. Robert W. Campbell and his wife, Dorothy, purchased the front tower in 1986 and had it moved closer to the riverbank near their home. Marie Eva Savage was the first private owner of the rear tower. When she passed away, it became the property of Joseph McKinnon. Gordon and Carla Burns purchased the tower in 2003 and had it moved eight kilometres east. In 2004 a deck and new red metal roof were added, and the tower was freshly painted in 2009.

Modern towers marked Grant Beach Range in 2011.

Travel Instructions: Take Route 11 to the northern side of the Miramichi River, and then continue east on Route 11 for 10 kilometres to the front tower in Lower Newcastle. Continue another 7.8 kilometres east for a view of the rear tower. The privately owned towers should only be viewed from the shoulder of Route 11.

Established: 1869 (current towers 1903)

Position: Front: 47.08226 N, -65.38593 W; Rear: 47.11209 N, -65.29233 W

Lights: Inactive

Tower Heights: Front: 11.3 metres; Rear 11.3 metres

Description: White square pyramidal towers, red lanterns

106. Sheldrake Island

Sheldrake Island Front Range tower. (Library and Archives Canada)

Sheldrake Island Rear Range tower. (Library and Archives Canada)

In 1873, a pair of beacon lights, consisting of lamps hoisted atop poles, was built on Sheldrake Island to lead mariners to the mouth of the Miramichi River. The front light was situated on the eastern end of the island, while the rear light was 3.6 kilometres away on the other side of the island. The first keeper, a Mr. Cameron, took sick shortly after becoming keeper and was replaced by John McKay, who was forced to sleep in a small shed meant for storing the lamps, as no dwelling had been provided.

In 1911, a 10.4-metre-tall square, wooden tower, surmounted by a square wooden lantern, was built to house the front light, and a 15.2-metre steel, skeletal tower, topped by a wooden lantern, was erected for the rear light. John J. Fitzgerald of Newcastle built these towers for $1,450. Sheldrake Range was decommissioned in 1952.

107. Grand Dune (Grandoon) Flats Range Front

Grand Dune Flats Lighthouse on station, 1922. (Library and Archives Canada)

Travel Instructions: From Highway 11 near Burnt Church, turn south onto Church River Road, drive 3.7 kilometres to the end, and make a left turn onto Bayview Drive. The lighthouse is on the left after a short distance and is easily viewed from the road without trespassing.

Established: 1916

Position: 47.19504 N, -65.13479 W

Light: Inactive

Tower Height: 11.6 metres

Description: White square dwelling, topped by red-roofed lantern

To enter Inner Miramichi Bay, mariners pass between Portage Island and Fox Island and then continue west to reach the Miramichi River. Roughly thirteen kilometres into the Inner Bay, vessels would pass between Grand Dune Island on their right and Point aux Carr on their left. The shallow area around Grand Dune Island was known as Grand Dune Flats and presented a hazard to navigation.

A dredge made a cut through Grand Dune Flats in 1884 to create Grand Dune Channel, and in 1916 range lights were constructed to mark the channel. The front light was displayed on the west end of Grand Dune Island from a square lantern centred atop the hipped roof of a square, two-storey keeper's dwelling, while the rear light shone from a steel skeletal tower on the mainland. Donald A. Ross was keeper of the lights from their establishment until at least 1934.

After the lights were decommissioned, the combination dwelling and front light was sold to Murray Anderson, who towed it across the ice to its current location in Burnt Church in the 1950s. (The structure last appeared in the *List of Lights* in 1956.) Anderson used the lighthouse as a summer cottage for several years before selling it to Ellen Kilbride in 1967.

Ellen Kilbride removed the gallery railing and enlarged a front window, and in the early 1990s, her son Terry added a carport with a wing above it to one side of the lighthouse. The lighthouse is the only one of its style remaining in New Brunswick.

The Grand Dune Flats Lighthouse with its new wing and supporting carport.

108. Hay Island

Hay Island Range Lights in 1928. (Canadian Coast Guard)

George Ingram erected range lights on Hay Island in 1881 to help vessels clear a shoal off the island. The front light was a lantern hoisted atop a mast, while the rear light, located sixty-four metres from the front, was shown from a square, pyramidal tower with a height of 6.4 metres. Joseph Allain replaced Joseph McKnight, the first keeper of the lights, in 1895 and built a dwelling at the station the following year.

In 1905, an enclosed pyramidal tower took the place of the pole light. The lights were discontinued in 1934.

109. Lower Neguac Range Rear (Tabusintac)

Though no longer active, Lower Neguac Range Rear Lighthouse was still in good condition in 2011.

Travel Instructions: From Highway 11 in Lower Neguac, turn south onto Rue Godin and drive 1 kilometre to its end. The lighthouse can be viewed from the wharf or by walking east along the beach.

Established: 1892 (present tower 1873)

Position: 47.26129 N, -65.05393 W

Light: Inactive

Tower Height: 10 metres

Description: White square pyramidal tower, red-roofed lantern

Located on the northeast side of Miramichi Bay, Neguac was settled by Jean Sovie in 1757. For years, the village depended on fishing and forestry, but today oyster farming and lobster fishing drive the local economy.

In 1891, tenders were invited to relocate the abandoned range lights at Tabusintac Gully to Lower Neguac. The main tower at Tabusintac was erected in 1873 on Crab Island, and a beacon light was later added to form range lights, but the lights were discontinued due to shallowing of the gully.

W. H. Noble moved the lights in October 1891 for $205.07, and Lower Neguac Range Lights commenced operation at the opening of navigation in 1892. The front light, consisting of a lantern hoisted atop a 4.9-metre-tall mast, was located on Lower Neguac Wharf, while the rear light was shown from the enclosed tower situated on the beach 320 metres away. In 1929, the rear light was relocated to a newly purchased site that placed it 366 metres from the front light.

Lower Neguac Rear Range Lighthouse was decommissioned in 2003, but an official light was still exhibited from Lower Neguac Wharf in 2011.

110. Neguac Gully

A string of barrier islands runs along the entrance to Inner Miramichi Bay, separated by a few narrow channels or gullies through which vessels may pass. In 1873, Neguac Gully Lighthouse was established on the southern end of the northernmost of these sandy islets to guide vessels through Neguac Gully.

The square, wooden tower commenced operation on August 20, 1873, with Farnham Letson as its keeper. Four flat-wick lamps and reflectors were employed in the lantern room to produce a fixed white light. In 1875, a pole light was established seaward of the lighthouse so mariners could align the two lights to safely enter the gully.

A dwelling house was added to the station in 1884. In 1929, an unwatched acetylene light exhibited from a red lantern atop a pole replaced the wooden tower.

Neguac Gully Range Lights with dwelling. (Library and Archives Canada)

Original Goose Lake Lighthouse. (Library and Archives Canada)

CHALEUR BAY

111. Goose Lake

A square, pyramidal tower with an attached dwelling was built near Goose Lake on the southwest coast of Miscou Island in 1874 and placed in operation the following April by Keeper J. B. Robichaux. The iron lantern atop the 8.5-metre tower housed a lighting apparatus with a circular-wick lamp and reflector on each of its two faces and revolved to produce a white flash every sixty seconds.

Drifting sand and an eroding shore were constant problems at the station. A storm in 1897 washed away the beach near the tower, necessitating the relocation of the oil house and the construction of a sea wall. In 1915, a fourth-order lens was mounted in the lantern room to produce a distinctive characteristic of ten seconds of light followed by a five-second eclipse. A pole light replaced the lighthouse in 1948 followed by a red skeletal tower, surmounted by a white wooden lantern, which served until 1967.

112. Harper Point (Miscou Harbour)

George Ingram erected a beacon light on Harper Point in 1887 to mark the western entrance to Miscou Harbour from Chaleur Bay. This navigational aid consisted of a small lantern hoisted atop a mast. In 1900, a taller mast was put in place, and a seventh-order lens was substituted for the original pressed glass lens.

A square, wooden tower with vertical sides commenced operation at Harper Point in 1911. Topped by a square lantern room, the tower sat atop a cribwork block

Harper Point Lighthouse before being relocated in 1922 to become Miscou Harbour Front Range. (Library and Archives Canada)

with pointed ends. In 1922, the tower was placed on a concrete foundation at a new site, where it served as the front light of the new Miscou Harbour Range. The rear light of this range was a headlight lantern shown from a pole. A skeletal tower replaced the wooden front tower in 1965.

113. Black Point

The Black Point Lighthouse in 2002. Since then the lower third of the central column has been removed.

Black Point Lighthouse, a skeletal tower with an enclosed central portion, was established in 1967. It is

Travel Instructions: Travelling north on Route 113 make a left onto Route 313 just before the bridge to Miscou Island. Continue 3.2 kilometres then turn right onto Chemin Light Road to reach the lighthouse.

Established: 1967

Position: 47.88439 N, -64.62361 W

Light: Yellow, on 4 s, eclipse 2 s, on 2 s, eclipse 2 s

Tower Height: 17.7 metres

Focal Plane: 17.6 metres

Description: Square skeletal tower, with enclosed central column and red lantern

the only lighthouse of its kind in New Brunswick and is still equipped with a fourth-order drum lens.

Formerly, the middle third of the square, central column was painted red, with the upper and lower thirds painted white. However, by 2009, the bottom third of the column's enclosure had been removed.

114. Marcelle Point

Marcelle Point Lighthouse seen here atop its wooden cribwork foundation. (Library and Archives Canada)

F. T. B. Young began construction of a square, wooden lighthouse in 1916 to mark the southeast tip of Pokesudie Island, known as Marcelle Point, but the 8.5-metre-tall tower was not completed until 1917. Young worked under a $450 contract, while the necessary land was expropriated for $83.

The lighthouse originally stood atop a cribwork foundation, 1.8 metres high, and in 1920 anchor bolts were put in place from the tower's corner posts to the wooden crib. In later years, the tower's foundation was a concrete base, located at the water's edge, and the lighthouse was accessed by an elevated wooden walkway. The tower was demolished in 1960 and replaced by a square skeletal tower surmounted by a red lantern.

115. Pokesudie

This tower served on Pokesudie Island for approximately one hundred years. (Library and Archives Canada)

Under a contract for $1,399, George Young constructed a square, wooden tower to mark the northeast corner of Pokesudie Island. The lighthouse stood 10.4 metres tall and was first lit on August 1, 1881, by Octave Hachey, who received an annual salary of $150.

A dwelling was built for the keeper in 1883, and in 1893, a seventh-order Chance lens replaced the tower's original lamps and reflectors. The original tower was discontinued around 1980. A square skeletal tower marked the point in 2011.

116. Caraquet Range Front 🚤 🛑
117. Caraquet Range Rear 🚗

Caraquet Front Range Lighthouse, with a vertical red range line on its seaward face, was still active in 2011.

Caraquet Rear Range Lighthouse, relocated and altered to serve a new purpose.

A pair of range lights, built under the direction of John Kelly, inspector of lights for New Brunswick, commenced operation on September 24, 1903, to lead vessels through Caraquet Channel and into the harbour at Bas-Caraquet. Both lighthouses are enclosed wooden towers, square in plan, with sloping sides and surmounted by square, wooden lanterns. The front tower stands close to the shore and originally displayed a fixed white light from a seventh-order lens. The rear tower, situated 1.2 kilometres inland, displayed a fixed white catoptric light.

Fred F. Doucett Jr. was hired as the first keeper of the front light, while Patrice L. Legere was the first keeper of the rear light.

In 2000, the Canadian Coast Guard erected an 11.3-metre-tall skeletal tower to serve as the rear light, and the 1903 tower was given to the town of Bas-Caraquet. The old tower was relocated 1.3 kilometres east, where it was refurbished and a roofed patio was attached. The lighthouse is now part of Les Chalets de la Plage de Bas-Caraquet, a community of seaside rental cottages.

Travel Instructions: From Route 145 in Bas Caraquet, drive north to the bay on Rue Lanteigne. The lighthouse is in Les Chalets de la Plage de Bas-Caraquet and guest parking is available outside the park. The front tower is surrounded by private property and best seen from the water.

Established: 1903

Position: Front: 47.80827 N, -64.84107 W; Rear: 47.80439 N, -64.82468 W

Light: Front: Fixed yellow; Rear: Inactive.

Tower Height: Front: 8.2 metres; Rear: 13.7 metres

Focal Plane: Front: 8.1 metres

Description: White square pyramidal towers, red-roofed lanterns. The front range has a red vertical stripe on its seaward face.

118. Caraquet Island

1870 Caraquet Island Lighthouse. (Provincial Archives of New Brunswick)

This photo of Caraquet Island Lighthouse was taken from the waterfront in Caraquet.

Caraquet Island parallels the shore near Middle Caraquet, providing protection for Caraquet Harbour. A combination lighthouse and dwelling, consisting of a rectangular, one-and-a-half-storey dwelling with a square tower rising from one end of its pitched roof, was erected on the western end of the island in 1870 by Daly and Carter of Miramichi at a cost of $548.

Keeper Thomas Kerr first exhibited the tower's fixed white light on August 26, 1870. Kerr's first wife, Ellen Young, passed away in 1847, leaving behind six children. The following year, Thomas married Mary Blackhall, and they had ten children, the last of whom was born after Kerr was appointed keeper at the age of fifty-seven.

On the night of October 14, 1872, Keeper Kerr's twenty-six-year-old son, Archibald, set out for Caraquet Island in a flat accompanied by John Ahern. The following morning, Keeper Kerr found the flat, bottom-up, near the island, but only after crossing to the mainland that afternoon did he learn that his son had tried to reach the island the previous evening. According to a newspaper account of the accident, Archibald was the fourth son that Thomas lost in the span of just a few short years.

On Friday, June 13 of the following year, Keeper Kerr travelled to the mainland to mail some papers related to the lighthouse. After finishing his business, he set off for the island in the afternoon aboard a "small leaky flat." The boat overturned, and Keeper Kerr perished. While men were dragging for his body the following day, they located the remains of Archibald, who had drowned in roughly the same location as his father.

Travel Instructions: A distant view of the lighthouse is possible from the waterfront in Caraquet.

Established: 1870 (present tower 1955)

Position: 47.82256 N, -64.90444 W

Light: White, on 1 s, eclipse 3 s

Tower Height: 20.1 metres

Focal Plane: 22.3 metres

Description: Rectangular skeletal tower, red lantern

Keeper Kerr's wife, Mary, assumed responsibility of the light for the remainder of the 1873 shipping season. With the opening of navigation in 1874, Narcisse Porlier started serving as keeper and was described by Inspector Mitchell that year as "a very efficient officer."

In late October 1876, Louis Porlier was appointed keeper in place of his father, Narcisse, who drowned near the island when a gale capsized the boat in which he and another son were fishing.

In 1885, the illuminating apparatus at Caraquet Island was changed to a dioptric light, and a storeroom and well were added to the station.

The present skeletal tower replaced the original lighthouse in 1955.

119. *Pointe à Brideau Range Rear*

Pointe à Brideau, New Brunswick's newest lighthouse, was built in 1991.

Travel Instructions: From Route 11 just west of where it intersects with Route 145 in Caraquet, take Rue Foley down to the shore.

Established: 1978

Position: 47.79507 N, -64.94160 W

Light: Fixed white

Tower Height: 12.8 metres

Focal Plane: 13.5 metres

Description: White square pyramidal tower with red vertical stripe on range line, red-roofed lantern

Skeletal range lights were established at Pointe à Brideau in 1978. Several years later, the town of Caraquet developed the beach area around the rear tower and received permission to construct a "wrapper" around the tower. The resulting lighthouse, built in 1991, is an accurate representation of an historic range tower. The town maintains the wooden shell, while the Coast Guard services the light.

120. Maisonnette

In 1915, S. Gammon built a combination dwelling and lighthouse on Pointe de Maisonnette under a contract for $2,700. This unique structure consisted of a square, two-storey residence, painted white, with a red, octagonal lantern centred on its hipped roof.

During the Second World War, Canadian military intelligence intercepted communications that exposed an elaborate German plan to liberate U-boat sailors from an Ontario prison camp. The prisoners were to tunnel their way out, cross Quebec, and rendezvous with a rescue party from U-536 at Pointe de Maisonnette. Only one escapee made it beyond the outskirts of the prison, and he managed to reach the pick-up point only to be arrested and taken to Maisonnette Lighthouse. Despite the presence of several Canadian warships, U-536 made it safely out of Chaleur Bay.

Maisonnette Lighthouse, 1940. (Jacques Godin)

Maisonnette Lighthouse was struck by lightning on August 9, 1946, and burned to the ground. A replacement light was soon established, and a square, skeletal tower marks the spot today.

Grand Anse Lighthouse was in operation for fifty years. (J-G. Landry)

121. Grande Anse

Many are familiar with the lighthouse painted in the colours of the Acadian flag that serves as a visitor information centre in Grande Anse. This structure is not historic, but the village did have an authentic lighthouse at one time.

In 1915, the George Eddy Company of Bathurst completed an 8.2-metre-tall tower that stood near the inner end of a breakwater in the village's boat harbour. This lighthouse served until 1965.

122. Stonehaven (Clifton Breakwater)

In 1878, the breakwater at Clifton was extended to form an artificial harbour to shelter fishing craft and schooners engaged in exporting grindstones. Richard Peters built a lighthouse at the shore end of the breakwater in 1885 under a contract for $620. This square, wooden tower stood 11.3 metres tall, was surmounted by an iron lantern, and displayed a fixed red light.

A fourth-order lens was mounted in the tower in 1916, and in 1923 a mast light was erected at the end of the wharf. The cast-iron lantern was removed from Stonehaven Lighthouse in 1929. A modern skeletal tower, located on the hill overlooking the wharf, was serving the harbour in 2011.

Stonehaven Lighthouse, 1963. (Canadian Coast Guard)

123. Belloni (Salmon) Point

Belloni Point Lighthouse, 1962. (Canadian Coast Guard)

In 1900, a square, wooden tower, measuring 6.7 metres tall, was constructed on Belloni Point, just east of Bathurst, to exhibit a fixed white light to indicate the outer limit of the shoal extending from the harbour. Robert Buttimer was hired as the first keeper at an annual salary of one hundred dollars. The tower last appeared on the *List of Lights* in 1972.

124. Bathurst Range

On April 21, 1871, range lights were established on Carron Point at a cost of $683 to mark the way into Bathurst Harbour. Both towers were hexagonal, with the front one showing a fixed white light and the rear one a fixed red light. John Conners was hired as their first keeper at an annual salary of $80.

In 1878, the rear tower was relocated to the site of the front light, and a new square wooden tower, painted in red and white stripes, was built to display the rear light. A new square, pyramidal tower, topped by a square wooden lantern, was erected in 1898 to take the place of the worn-out front tower. In 1915, a pole light, distant 3.8 kilometres from the front light, was erected to serve as the rear light. Previously, the two range lights were separated by just 110 metres. The front, wooden tower was used until 1970. Modern skeletal towers were in use at Carron Point in 2011.

Bathurst Front Range Light, 1933. (Library and Archives Canada)

125. Petit Rocher

Joseph Morrison was awarded a contract in 1878 to erect a square, wooden lighthouse on Elm Tree Point in Petit Rocher. The tower stood 9.4 metres tall, and Keeper Hilarion Roy first lit its fixed white light on May 24, 1879.

A wharf was built at Petit Rocher in 1908, and in 1912 a pole light was established on the wharf's outer end. Around this time, the wooden tower was cut into pieces and removed from the point.

Petit Rocher Lighthouse served on Elm Tree Point for roughly thirty-three years. (Library and Archives Canada)

126. Belledune Point
127. Little Belledune Point

Little Belledune Lighthouse, 1946. (Canadian Coast Guard)

Belledune Point Lighthouse on the grounds of the smelting plant just prior to being moved. (Charles Stewart)

During the early history of Belledune, its residents relied on farming, fishing, and lumbering. Another industry arrived in 1963 when Brunswick Mining and Smelting Corporation began work on a $30-million smelter, fed partially by mines established near Bathurst in the 1950s. The plant opened in 1966, and two years later an adjacent port was completed.

In 1972, the Canadian Coast Guard established an automated navigational aid on Belledune Point to help vessels calling at the new port. Square, pyramidal, and 10.7 metres tall, Belledune Point Lighthouse stood on the point until 2002, when Charles Stewart acquired the tower and cut it up into three pieces, which he moved to Seaside. The Coast Guard replaced the wooden tower with a square skeletal tower. Stewart planned to reassemble the tower on his bayside property, but as of 2011, the individual pieces were still awaiting restoration.

Long before Belledune Point Lighthouse was constructed, a similarly named light commenced operation on Little Belledune Point, 5.3 kilometres to the west. The original Little Belledune Light, first exhibited on June 10, 1884, was a simple light hoisted up a

mast. George Ingram was paid ninety-five dollars for erecting the beacon, and William Roherty was hired as its first keeper. In 1907, an octagonal, wooden tower, surmounted by an iron lantern, was constructed on the point by Samuel Gammon of Bathurst to replace the mast light. A wooden, two-storey keeper's dwelling was completed the following year. A fourth-order revolving lens, formerly used on Georgian Bay, was installed in Little Belledune Lighthouse and produced a white light interrupted by a brilliant flash every thirty seconds.

Before being decommissioned in 1971, Little Belledune Lighthouse was in operation for eighty-eight years and was kept exclusively by members of the Roherty family. For this reason, the lighthouse was known as Roherty Lighthouse. After William Roherty, the first keeper, drowned in a fishing accident in 1895, his sister Ann took charge of the light. Ann was assisted by her nephew James, who became the official keeper in 1905. After the Second World War, James was succeeded by his son James Alton, who had served in the military during the conflict. Besides caring for the light, James Alton raised a family of six children with his wife, Mildred, and served as the first mayor of Belledune.

Amid some controversy, it was decided in 1976 that Roherty Lighthouse would be relocated and used as a tourist information office, but the day before the move, it was destroyed in a suspicious fire.

128. Heron Island

In the early 1800s, Heron Island was divided into twelve parcels that became home to families who made a living by fishing and keeping small farms. In 1874, a square, wooden tower, measuring 6.1 metres tall, was built on the island's north shore to guide vessels to and from Dalhousie.

Keeper John Dutch lit the tower's three flat-wick lamps for the first time on April 1, 1875. During an inspection that year, it was noted that the "building was not in order, the keeper knowing nothing about trimming lamps, or any other duty connected with the light, having never received any instruction from any person capable of showing him his duty." The inspector thought Dutch "was very anxious to learn his duty, and will probably succeed," and this proved to be true, as two years later, the inspector reported, "Mr. Dutch, is a very good officer, and understands his duty." An octagonal lantern and a fifth-order French lens were placed atop the tower in 1908, and the following year, a "wooden shelter shed" was built near the lighthouse.

In 1921, Stella LaPointe noticed an advertisement for a lighthouse keeper and postmaster on Heron Island. She urged her husband, George, to apply, and he begrudgingly agreed, but only if Stella would submit the application. George got the job and moved his wife and daughter into a small dwelling near the lighthouse. A veteran of the First World War, George faithfully kept the light while raising eleven children on the island. The dwelling at the lighthouse was soon too small, so George built a house near the wharf on the opposite side of the

Heron Island Lighthouse, circa 1950. (Allan Roy)

island. After the Second World War broke out, Keeper LaPointe felt compelled to resign and once again defend his country. In 2009, descendants of George and Stella LaPointe returned to Heron Island and erected a stone cairn in memory of the nineteen years George and Stella kept the lighthouse.

A metal tower replaced the original lighthouse in 1950, and a modern beacon marked the island in 2011.

129. Dalhousie Wharf 🚗 🛑
130. Douglas Island

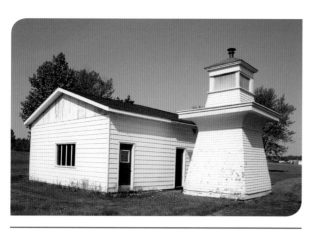

Privately owned Dalhousie Wharf Lighthouse, 2011.

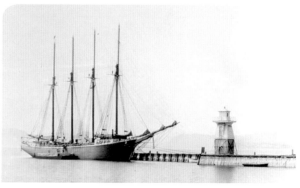

1909 Dalhousie Wharf Light with schooner. (Library and Archives Canada)

In the 1870s, Dalhousie Harbour was defined on the east by Douglas Island and on the west by Montgomery Island. Both of these islets were connected to shore by a spit and between them vessels could anchor in twelve metres of water.

An appropriation of $800 was made in 1879 to construct range lights at Dalhousie, Campbellton, and Oak Point on the Quebec shore to guide vessels along the Restigouche River. Peter Naduux of Dalhousie was awarded a $762 contract for constructing the six needed towers.

The front light at Dalhousie was placed on the public wharf, while the rear light was shown from Montgomery Island. In 1884, a freight shed was built on the wharf, and a lantern was placed atop it to serve as the front light. A square wooden tower with a height of 6.7 metres was established on Douglas Island in 1886.

In 1905, Douglas Island Lighthouse was replaced by an octagonal wooden tower erected on the northern point of the island. The tower stood 16.2 metres tall and employed a fifth-order dioptric lens to produce a bright flash every 7.5 seconds. Patrick B. Troy of Dalhousie constructed the tower at a cost of $1,642.

In 1909, Patrick B. Troy also built a seven-metre wooden lighthouse tower on the Government Wharf for $645.02, and the lights atop the freight shed and on Montgomery Island were discontinued. A steel framework was placed beneath the tower around 1910 to increase the height of the light.

In 1879, seventy-one-year-old Malcom McNeill petitioned for the position of keeper of the soon-to-be-completed range lights at Dalhousie. Malcolm was awarded the job, but decided his son, Henry Havelock McNeill, was better suited for the work. Keeper Henry McNeill started at an annual salary of one hundred dollars and tended the lights on Dalhousie Wharf and Douglas Island until 1930.

In 1960, John Audet placed a winning bid of twenty-five dollars for the decommissioned Dalhousie Wharf Lighthouse after seeing a notice posted in a local store. Workers who were dismantling the wharf took the lighthouse down off its supports, and Audet had the small tower trucked to his property.

The lighthouse has been maintained in excellent condition over the years with Mr. Audet building interior stairs and securing a modern lens for the lantern room in 2009. Audet wanted the community of

Douglas Island Lighthouse moments before being severely damaged. (Bill Clarke)

Charlo to take over the tower, but this plan seems to have faltered.

In 1974, Douglas Island Lighthouse was discontinued to make room for a cargo wharf on the island. The octagonal tower was going to be burned, but Jack Macdonald fought to save the lighthouse, and the town requested that the contractors move the structure to a temporary location. On February 22, 1974, a crane lifted the five-ton lighthouse into the air, and with the tower dangling from its boom, proceeded off the island. As the crane passed over a rough patch of ground, the tower started to sway causing the crane to rock dangerously. The operator quickly lowered the tower, and when he went to pick it up again, one of the cable clamps gave way. The lighthouse plummeted to the rocks below and toppled over, shattering its lantern room and the upper portion of the tower.

Due to the prohibitive cost of repairs, the lighthouse was scrapped.

It was estimated that Douglas Island Lighthouse could have generated ten thousand dollars in tourist income each year. The return of Dalhousie Wharf Light might not generate as much money, but it would make an attractive addition to the city's waterfront.

131. Inch Arran (Bon Ami)

The unusual "birdcage" lantern on the Inch Arran Lighthouse is the only one of its kind remaining in the province.

Immigrants from Scotland's Isle of Arran named the point protruding eastward into Chaleur Bay at Dalhousie Inch Arran after their native home. (Inch is Gaelic for Island.) Just offshore from the point are Bon Ami Rocks, named after Peter Bonamie, an early settler of the area.

Inch Arran Point has also been known as Bonami Point, and there is another name it has had—Arseneau Point. In the 1800s, the Arseneau family lived nearby, and Marie-Louise Arseneau would place a candle, and later a lamp, in her window to guide her husband, sons, and other local fishermen back home in the night. Marie-Louise looked after not only the fishermen but also the sick, for she was known as the medicine-woman of Dalhousie. Using her knowledge of herbs and roots, she would treat the infirm, some of whom came from afar to seek her help.

In 1870, the current Inch Arran Lighthouse, an eleven-metre-tall, square, wooden tower, was built on the point. The tower's fixed white light, produced by a No.1 circular-wick lamp, two flat-wick lamps, and three fifteen-inch reflectors, was exhibited for the first time on November 7, 1870, by Louis Arseneau, Marie-Louise's husband.

Louis Arseneau passed away in April of 1888, and his grandson Joseph Arseneau assumed responsibility for the lighthouse. In 1901, Keeper Arseneau requested a raise as he was making only one hundred dollars a year, the same amount given to his grandfather in 1870. "My neighbour Light House Keeper John Dutch of Heron Island gets Five Hundred a year," Arseneau informed the department. "If it was not for the light I could earn fair wages in summer working on ships, but it binds one at home."

In response, the deputy minister of marine and fisheries wrote:

I have to inform you that as your light is an unimportant harbour light and the salary the same as paid to other keepers of similar harbour lights no increase can be allowed you at present. I have also to inform you that when a keeper receives a salary such as is paid you the Department does not expect him to give all his time to the duties of lightkeeper, and as your light is close to a village you should be able to obtain additional employment.

Travel Instructions: From Route 11, take Exit 391 and drive north on Darlington Drive. Continue on Darlington Drive, which will become Renfrew Street, for 4.3 kilometres, and then turn right on Victoria Street, which terminates at the lighthouse.

Established: 1870

Position: 48.06083 N, -66.35107 W

Light: White, on 3 s, off 3 s

Tower Height: 10.9 metres

Focal Plane: 13.7 metres

Description: White square pyramidal tower, red birdcage lantern

Joseph Arseneau passed away in November of 1913, and his wife, Denise, was made temporary keeper of the light until the close of navigation that year. W. S. Montgomery, Member of Parliament, recommended that Denise Arseneau be retained as keeper as her property was near the light, and any other caretaker would live at least a kilometre away.

In 1972, Inch Arran Lighthouse became a front range light when a metal skeletal tower was erected a few hundred metres to the west to help mariners enter the Restigouche River.

Under the Federal Heritage Buildings Policy, Inch Arran Lighthouse was recognized as a Federal Heritage Building on September 5, 1991, partly for the unusual "birdcage" of iron bars that surrounds the lantern.

132. Campbellton

Early Campbellton Range Light, 1899. (Library and Archives Canada)

This tower was built by the city of Campbellton in 1985 and is a member of Hostelling International.

George Cummings was the first keeper of the Campbellton Range Lights, built in 1879 by Peter Naduux of Dalhousie. The front light was displayed from the railway wharf. In 1895, the companion rear tower was moved from Moffat's Wharf to Kilgour Shive's wharf. The colour of the range lights was changed from fixed white to fixed red in 1898 to distinguish from other lights used nearby.

By 1917, the original rear tower had been replaced by a light on a pole. Utilitarian square, steel towers later replaced the wooden front tower and the rear pole light.

In 1985, the city of Campbellton received permission to occupy the land surrounding the rear light and incorporated the steel, skeletal tower into an octagonal lighthouse with an attached dwelling that now operates as Campbellton Lighthouse Hostel. Campbellton may have lost its historic lighthouses, but at least visitors to the city today can find clean, inexpensive accommodations in a modern lighthouse.

Travel Instructions: From Route 11 in Campbellton, take Exit 412 and drive north, towards the river, on Salmon Boulevard Extension. When this road ends, turn left onto Ramsay Street and then make a left just before the river onto Water Street. After a few blocks, make a right onto Ritchie Street, which ends at the hostel.

Established: 1879 (present tower 1985)

Position: 48.01002 N, -66.67201 W

Light: Fixed yellow

Tower Height: 16.5 metres

Focal Plane: 17.2 metres

Description: White octagonal tower with red vertical stripe on range line, red-roofed lantern

Glossary

catoptric: A light that uses a concave mirror for magnification. Often indicated in List of Lights as "C." They were common before widespread use of Fresnel lenses but continued in some lighthouses long after.

characteristic: The unique identity of a lighthouse, including the light exhibited and the fog alarm sounded, that allows mariners to distinguish one lighthouse from another.

cornice: Ornamental overhang often found on lighthouses as a graceful decorative treatment below the lantern or gallery deck. May be a simple sweeping curve or may include decorative elements such as ornamental brackets. Example: Cape Jourimain.

daymark: The features and markings of a lighthouse visible during daytime.

decommissioned: A lighthouse that no longer functions as a navigational aid.

de-staffed: An automated lighthouse that has had its resident or non-resident keeper removed. Also known as "unwatched."

diaphone: A powerful type of foghorn invented in Canada that produced a loud "blast" followed by a "grunt." It used compressed air generated by a steam, gas, or oil engine, usually housed in its own building.

dioptric: A light that uses a lens for magnification. This is usually a Fresnel lens with size often indicated in List of Lights as "D" (D,6 = sixth-order).

fixed: A continuous steady light.

flashing: A light that appears at regular intervals with the light period being shorter than the period of darkness, or eclipse.

focal plane: Height of a light above the surface of the water in an active lighthouse. This book includes the former focal planes for those decommissioned lighthouses still in their original positions.

Fresnel: The lens invented by Augustin Fresnel in 1821 which consists of concentric ridges radiating outward from the central lens (bull's-eye), with prisms positioned at the top and bottom of the ridges to refract the light from the light source placed behind the central lens. A term normally used only when referring to traditional-cut, glass-style lenses, although the Fresnel principle is also found in more modern glass or plastic lenses.

gallery: Exterior walkway around the lantern.

group flashing: A flashing light that combines flashes in groups of two or more, creating its own unique pattern or signal. Used to avoid confusion where several lighthouses are in close proximity.

lamp: The lighting apparatus inside the lens (e.g. oil lamp, kerosene vapor burner, electric light bulb).

lantern: The exterior enclosure that protects the lens and lamp. Often confused with the lens or lamp, it is actually the top portion of the lighthouse from the deck up.

lens: Any glass or transparent material that is shaped to concentrate, magnify, and focus light.

lighthouse: Enclosed tower originally designed with an enclosed lantern and built by a governing authority as an aid to navigation.

lightstation: Light tower and associated buildings (dwellings, sheds, boathouses, fog alarm, etc.) and the land they occupy. In New Brunswick these include Cape Enrage, Gannet Rock, Green's Point, Head Harbour, Machias Seal Island, and Swallowtail.

list of lights: Official government list of navigational aids along the coasts and inland waterways featuring brief descriptions and precise locations.

navigational aid/aid to navigation: Devices and structures used to assist navigation by mariners, which includes but is not limited to lighthouses. May also include buoys, radio beacons, fog alarms, etc.

occulting: A light that appears at regular intervals briefly interrupted by periods of darkness, which are shorter than the period of light.

order: A measurement of the size of a Fresnel lens, with first-order being the most powerful (and largest) and seventh-order being the least powerful (and smallest).

Types of Lighthouses

coastal light: A medium-sized lighthouse marking major coastal features, such as capes, points, and major islands. Example: Point Escuminac.

harbour light: A small lighthouse used to assist navigation within a harbour. Sometimes located on wharves or piers in which case they are known as wharf or pier lights. Example: Cape Tormentine Outer Wharf.

hazard avoidance light: A lighthouse used to mark a specific hazard, such as a shoal, reef, rocky point, or dangerous island. Many lighthouses serve as both coastal and hazard avoidance lights. Example: Gannet Rock.

landfall light: A large lighthouse first sighted as a mariner nears land. There are no such lights in New Brunswick.

leading light: A lighthouse used as a landmark when fixing a course along a waterway. More commonly found as inland lights. Example: Sand Point, St. John River.

range lights: A pair of lights that indicate a safe course when lined up one above the other. Sometimes one or both may be displayed from simple skeletal towers, but older range lights can often be fine heritage structures. Example: Point-du-Chêne.

Lighthouse Architecture

concrete octagonal: Eight-sided tapering tower made of concrete, which continues a traditional wooden style in a more permanent material. Example: Musquash Head.

concrete square: A four-sided non-tapering light tower of concrete construction, usually with an attached square foghorn building. Example: Quaco Head.

pyramidal: A term used here that encompasses any tapered lighthouse usually—but not always—with a separate lantern. Example: Pointe à Jérôme front.

round fibreglass: A round, tapering tower made of fibreglass, utilizing lightweight prefabricated material that retains a traditional lighthouse style. Example: Cape Spencer.

salt shaker: A popular term for the smaller square, tapered style of lighthouse, usually with a square lantern. Roughly resembling the proportions of a salt shaker, hence the term. Example: Anderson Hollow.

skeletal tower: An open steel or aluminum tower not generally considered a heritage structure but may occupy the site of an historic lighthouse. Example: Black Point.

square tapered: Four-sided structure that in the Maritimes is almost always made of wood. Can be of dramatically varying heights. Example: Portage Island.

tapered: Inwardly sloping walls used on most lighthouses to provide strength and stability and to lessen wind resistance.

wooden octagonal: Eight-sided structure, usually tapering lighthouse tower constructed of wood. Example: Swallowtail.

wooden square: A four-sided, non-tapering light tower of wood construction, more common along inland waterways. Example: Hampstead.

Bibliography

Annual Report of the Department of Marine, various years.

Sessional Papers of the Dominion of Canada, various years.

Journal of the House of Assembly of the Province of New Brunswick, various years.

Official Report of the Debates of the House of Commons of the Dominion of Canada, 1907–1908.

Adams, Harold W. J. "Grant Beach lighthouses were first lighted back in 1869—133 years ago." *Miramichi Leader*, March 22, 2002.

Bligh, R. W. *The New York Herald Almanac and Financial, Commercial, and Political Register for 1874*. New York Herald, 1874.

"Canoe to Steamboat: St. John River Travel." York Sunbury Museum, Fredericton, New Brunswick.

Carr, Deborah. "The Light with an Image to Keep." *Atlantic Co-operator*, May 2005.

D'Entremont, Jeremy. "Canada's St. Andrews Lighthouse on the Road to Restoration," *Lighthouse Digest*, October 2003.

D'Entremont, Jeremy. "Cape Enrage Lighthouse: An ongoing success story," *Lighthouse Digest*, January 2001.

Denys, Nicolas. "Description and Natural History of the Coasts of North America (Acadia)," *The Nautical Magazine*, 1887.

Dines, Prescott. "Reminiscences of a lighthouse keeper," *St. Croix Courier*, July 2, 1980.

"Government of Canada transfers ownership of Hendry Farm Lighthouse to Village of Cambridge-Narrows," Department of Fisheries and Ocean News Release, September 23, 2005.

Hadley, Michael L. and Roger Sarty. *Tin-pots and Pirate Ships*. McGill-Queen's University Press, 1991.

"Historic Structure Destroyed," *Telegraph-Journal*, February 25, 1974.

Ingersoll, L. K. *On This Rock, An Island Anthology*, Gerrish House Society, 1963.

Klinkenberg, Marty. "150-year-old lighthouse feted at Grand Manan celebration," *Telegraph-Journal*, July 8, 2010.

Klinkenberg, Marty. "Home is a beacon for lighthouse man of Neguac," *Telegraph-Journal*, August 7, 2009.

Larsen, G. Christian. "William Andrew Murray: A Pea Point Lighthouse Keeper"

"Lighthouse Burned," *Boston Daily Globe*, February 15, 1911.

Loughery, Kelly Anne. "Southern New Brunswick Lighthouse Divestiture," *Lighthouse Digest*, September 2008.

Macdonald, Copthorne. *Bridging the Strait*, Dundurn Press, 1997.

MacDonald, David. "Up the Cliff: The Vernon Bagley Rescue," *Reader's Digest*, March 1968.

MacDonald, Myron. *Richibucto River of Fire*, 1989.

MacLennan, Mrs. K. Bliss. "Escuminac Point Lighthouse," 1965.

Marine File No. 20007K, South West Head Grand Manan Light, Library and Archives Canada.

Marine File No. 20010-5C, Long Point White Head Island, Library and Archives Canada.

Marine File No. 20010K, Long Point White Head Island, Library and Archives Canada.

Mills, Chris. "Kathleen Ingersoll: At Home on Gannet Rock," *Lighthouse Digest*, April 2004.

"North America's Most Endangered Lighthouse," *Lighthouse Digest*, May 1999.

Perley, Moses Henry. *Report on the Sea and River Fisheries of New Brunswick*, 1852.

Robichaud, Jesse. "Lighthouses' future uncertain in N.B.," *Times and Transcript*, June 7, 2010.

Snell, M. S. *Essays, short stories, and poems*, Chatam, 1881.

Soucoup, Dan. *McCully's New Brunswick: historic aerial photographs, 1931–1939*, Dundurn Press, 2005.

U.S. Hydrographic Office. *The Gulf and River St. Lawrence*, Washington Government Printing Office, 1908

"Vicious Storm Causes Heavy Loss of Life," *Canadian Fisherman*, August 1959.

Welles, Darrell. "The History of Green's Point Light," August 18, 1997. http://www.greenspoint.canadianwebs. com/history2.htm

Weston, Wainwright 'Pappy'. *Stories About Me and People I Have Known*, Quebecor World Atlantic, 2000.

Index

Anderson Hollow	86	Great Duck Island	16	Partridge Island	49
Barnes Point	95	Green's Point (L'etete Passage)	35	Pea Point	41
Bathurst Range	143	Grindstone Island	89	Pecks Point	94
Bayswater	66	Gull Cove	15	Petit Rocher	143
Belledune Point	144	Hampstead Wharf	73	Point Escuminac	114
Belloni (Salmon) Point	142	Harper Point (Miscou Harbour)	135	Point Lepreau	44
Belyeas Point	68	Hay Island	131	Pointe à Brideau Range Rear	140
Big Shippegan	120	Head Harbour (East Quoddy)	24	Pointe à Jérôme Range Front	110
Black Point	136	Hendry Farm	74	Pointe à Jérôme Range Rear	110
Bliss Island	37	Heron Island	145	Pointe du Chêne Range Front	103
Bouctouche (Buctouche) Bar	107	Hopewell Wharf	92	Pointe du Chêne Range Rear	103
Bridges Point	79	Inch Arran (Bon Ami)	148	Pointe Sapin	113
Caissie Point	105	Indian Point Range Front	97	Pokemouche Island	118
Campbellton	150	Indian Point Range Rear	97	Pokesudie	137
Cape Enrage	83	Jemseg	76	Portage Island	118
Cape Jourimain	101	Leonardville	27	Preston Beach	125
Cape Spencer	56	Lighthouse Point (Drew's Head/		Quaco Head	58
Cape Tormentine Outer Wharf	99	Beaver Harbour)	43	Reed's Point (The Three Sisters	
Cape Tormentine Range Rear	99	Little Belledune Point	144	Lamp)	55
Caraquet Island	139	Long Eddy Point (Grand Manan)	19	Richibucto Beach	112
Caraquet Range Front	138	Long Point	14	Richibucto Head (Cap Lumière)	111
Carquet Range Rear	138	Lower Musquash Island	74	Robertson Point	77
Chamcook	34	Lower Neguac Range Rear		Saint John Coast Guard Base	53
Chance Harbour	46	(Tabusintac)	132	Saint John Harbour Beacon	52
Cherry Island	26	Machias Seal Island	5	Sand Point	67
Cocagne Range Front	106	Maisonnette	141	Seal Cove Breakwater	12
Cox Point	77	Marcelle Point	137	Shamper's Wharf	72
Dalhousie Wharf	146	Mark Point	29	Shediac Island	104
Digby Pier	54	Martin Head	83	Shediac Wharf	104
Dipper Harbour	46	McColgan Point	65	Sheldrake Island	129
Dixon Point Range Front	108	McFarlane Point	93	South Tracadie	117
Dixon Point Range Rear	108	McMann Point	79	Southwest Head	10
Douglas Island	139	Midjik Bluff	34	Southwest (Southern) Wolf Island	21
Fanjoys Point	77	Miscou Island	122	Spruce Point	29
Fort Folly Point	92	Mulholland Point	22	St. Andrews (Pendlebury)	30
Fort Monckton	97	Musquash Head	47	St. Martins Breakwater	61
Fox Island Ranges	126	Navy Bar	32	St. Martins Visitor Information	
Gagetown	75	Negro Point	48	Centre	60
Gannet Rock	7	Neguac Gully	133	Stonehaven (Clifton Breakwater)	142
Glenwood	69	Newcastle (Lime Kiln Bank)	127	Swallowtail	17
Goose Lake	135	North Tracadie	117	Swift Point (Green Head)	64
Grand Dune Flats Range Front	130	Oak Point	71	The Cedars	69
Grand Harbour (Ross Island)	12	Oak Point Range Front	127	Tongue Shoal (Sand Reef)	33
Grande Anse	141	Oromocto Shoals	80	Wilmot Bluff	80
Grant Beach Range Front	128	Outhouse Point	93		
Grant Beach Range Rear	128	Palmer's Landing	72		